Elementary Music Theory © 2023 by San Marco Publications. All rights reserved.

All right reserved. No part of this book may be reproduced in any form or by electronic or mechanical means including Information storage and retrieval systems without permission in writing from the author.

ISNB: 1-896499-45-7

Contents

Lesson 1:	Pitch and Notation	3
Lesson 1:	Time Values	5
Lesson 3:	Accidentals	6
Lesson 4:	Major Scales	11
Lesson 5:	Minor Scales	17
Lesson 6:	Other Scales	24
Lesson 7:	C Clefs	29
Lesson 8:	Modes	32
Lesson 9:	Intervals	33
Lesson 10:	Meter 1	42
Lesson 11:	Chords	54
Lesson 12:	Cadences	66
Lesson 13:	Meter 2	76
Lesson 14:	Transposition	91
Lesson 15:	Score Types	98
Lesson 16:	Melody	100
Lesson 17:	Music Analysis	112

Essential Music Theory Complete Answers
Lesson 1 - Pitch and Notation

Page 9, No. 1

F D B A E E
G F C A B D
E D C B A G
F E A F C D

Page 11, No. 1

B G E D A A
G F C A B D
A G F E D C
A G C A E F

Page 13, No. 1

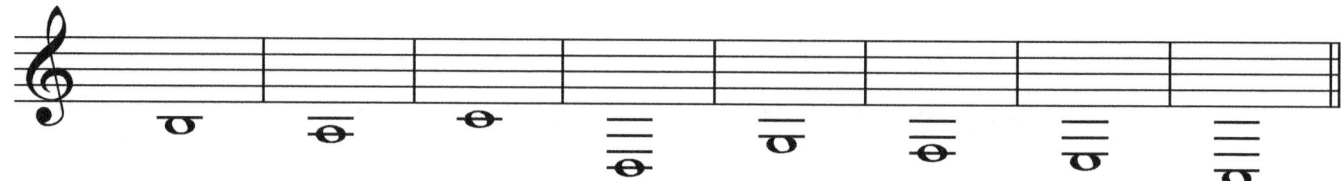

Page 13, No. 2

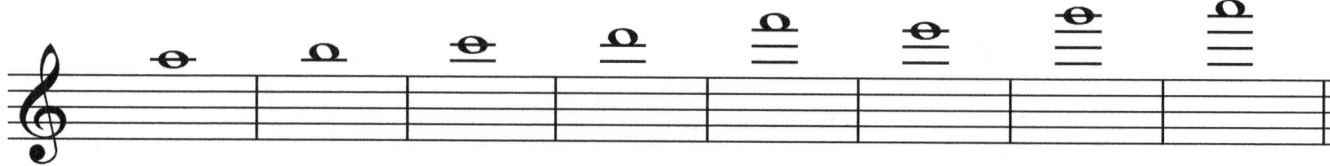

Page 13, No.3

Page 13, No.4

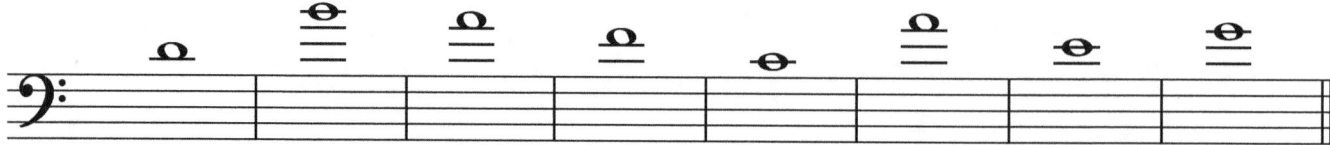

© San Marco Publications 2018

Page 14, No.1

F C F B A D E C
E D B F G A C C

Page 15, No. 3

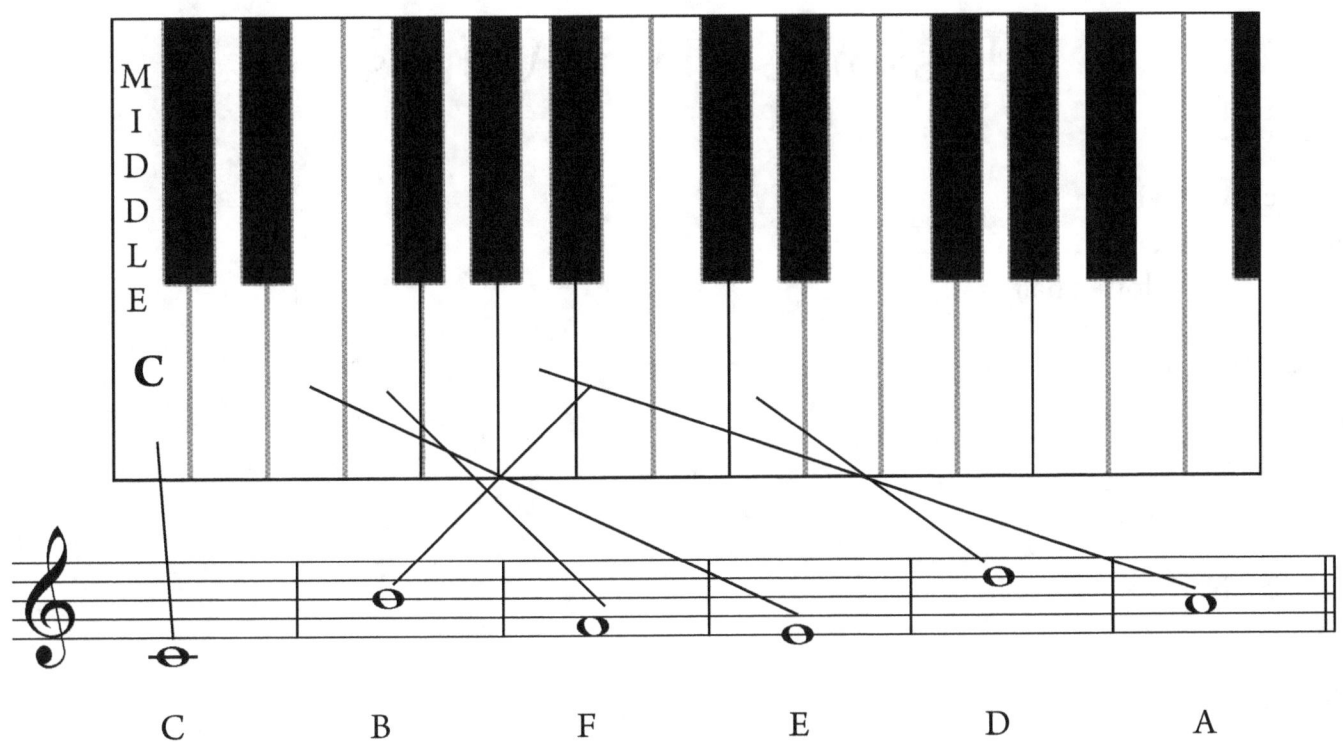

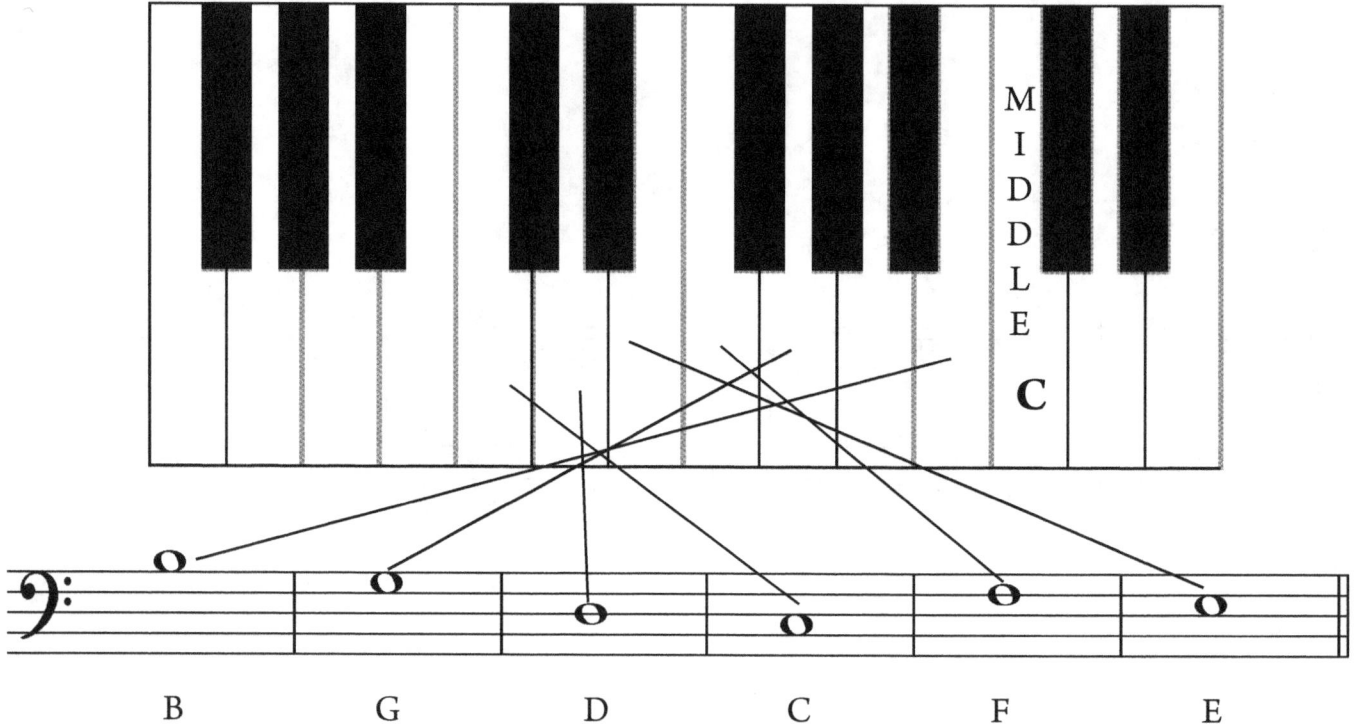

Lesson 2 - Time Values

Page 19, No. 1

quarter	eighth
half	eighth
whole	dotted half

Page 19, No. 2

1	1
2	4
1/2	3

Page 20, No. 3

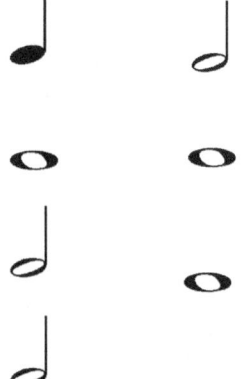

Page 21, No. 1

Page 24, No. 5

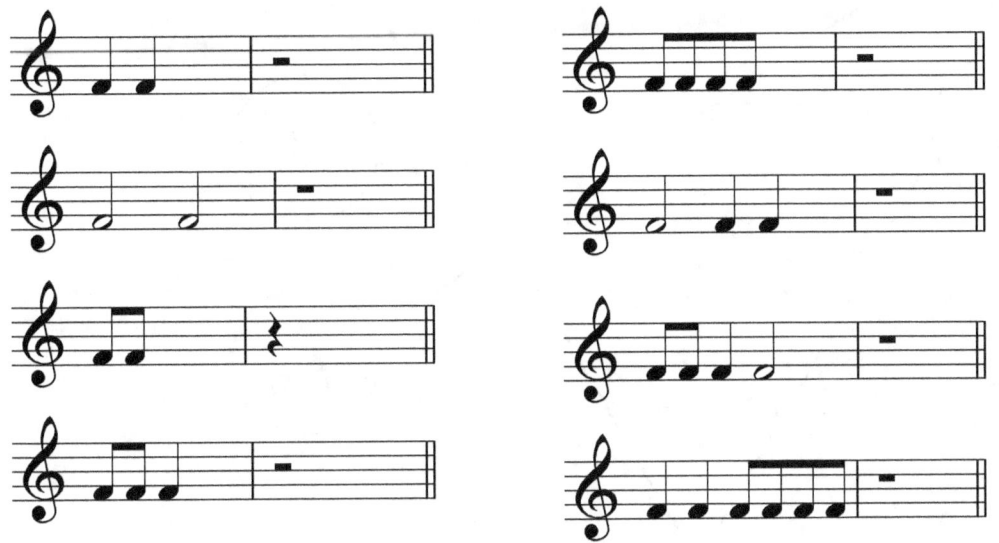

Page 24, No. 6

F	E	A	D	C	G	A	B	G
4	1	2	1/2	1/2	1	1/2	2	1/2

Lesson 3 - Accidentals

Page 27, No. 1 other answers are possible

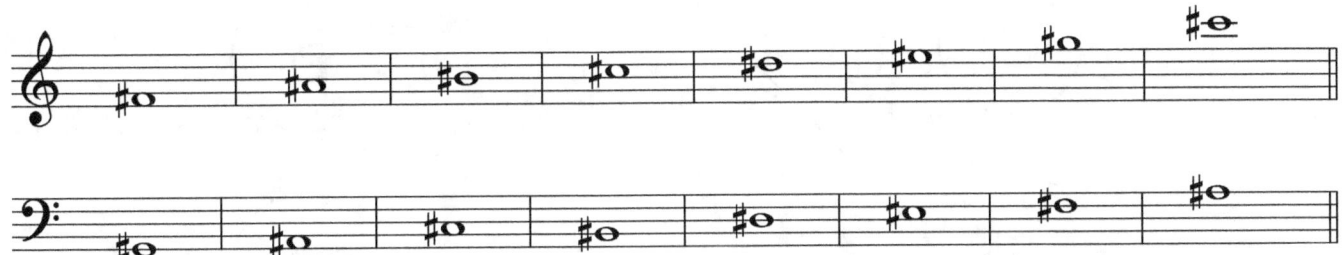

© San Marco Publications 2018

Page 28, No. 2 other answers are possible

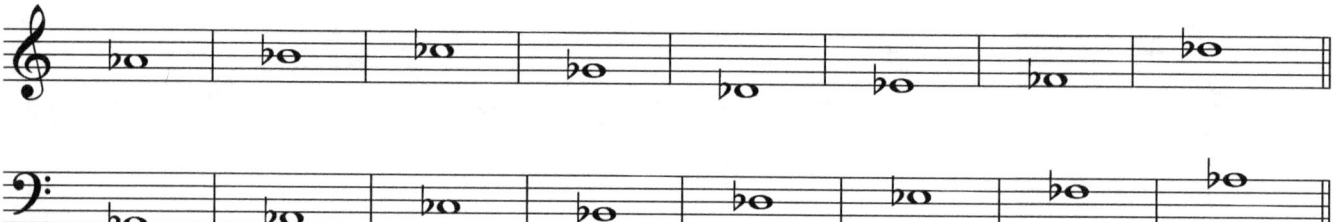

Page 30, No. 3

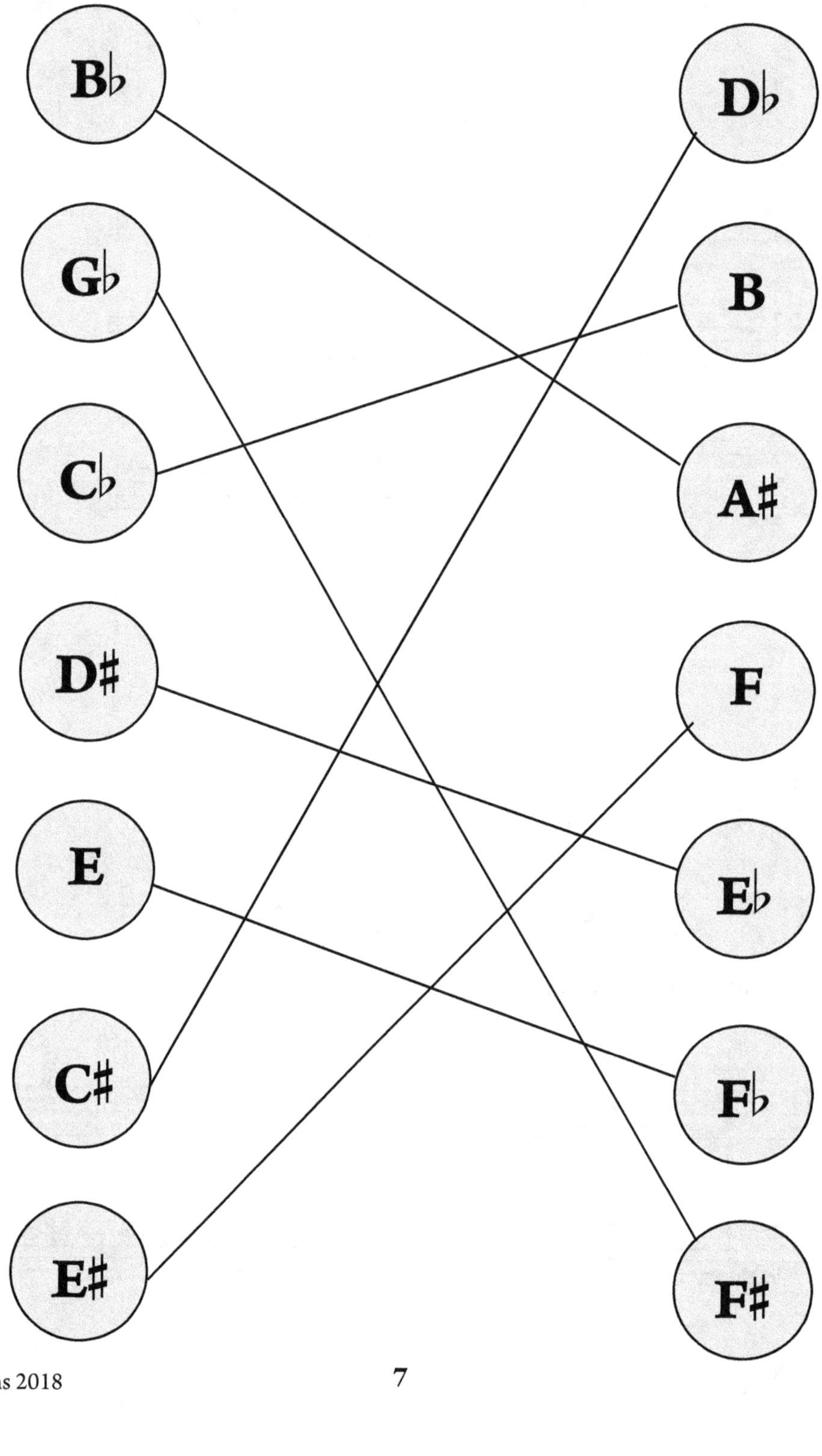

Page 32, No. 1

F# E F# C# D A B♭ E♭ E F# E D

A♭ C E♭ A G# E G B B♭ D B♭ F#

Page 32, No. 2, other options are possible

Page 32, No. 3, other options are possible

Page 33, No. 4, other options are possible

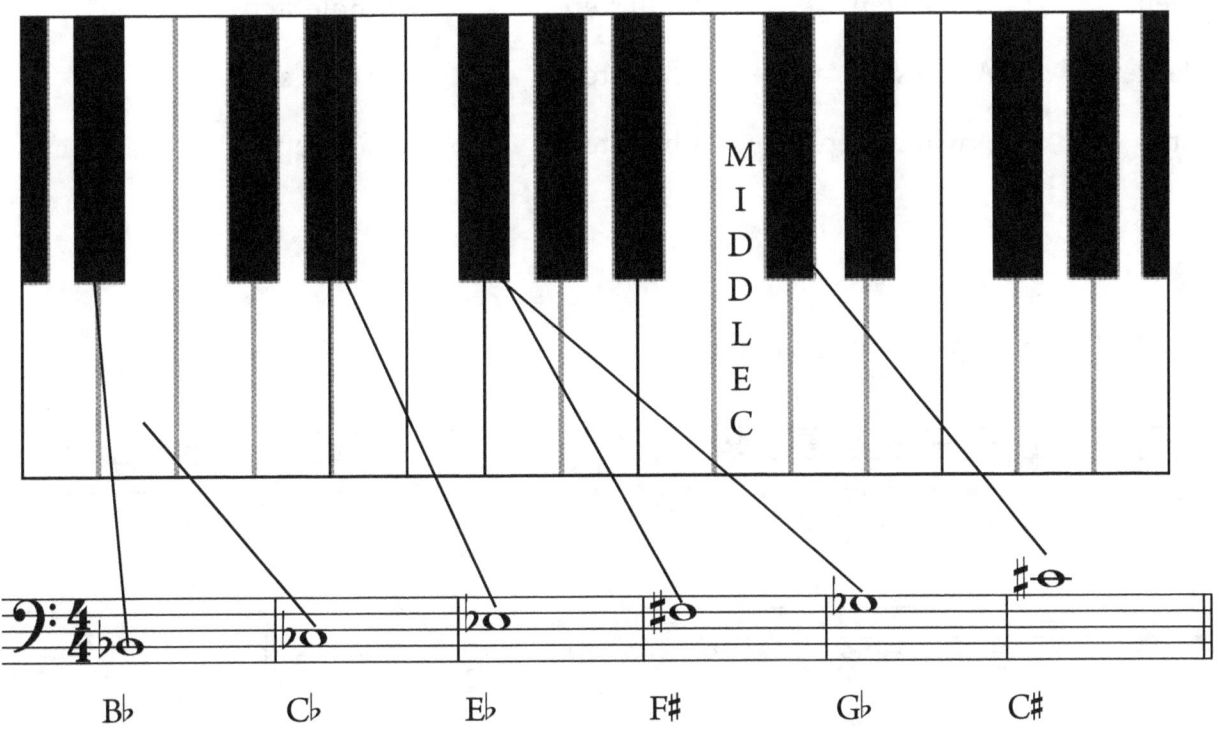

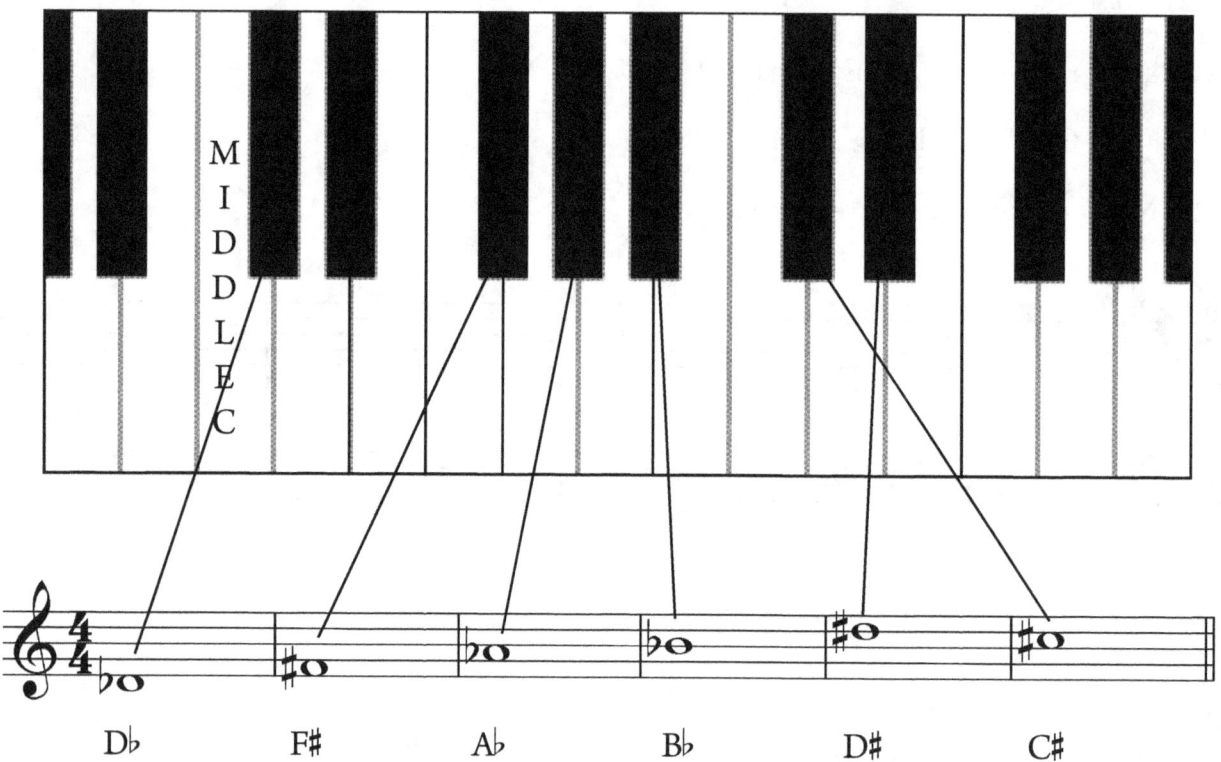

Page 34, No. 5

A whole step	A half step	A whole step	A whole step
A half step	A half step	A half step	A whole step
A whole step	A half step	A half step	A whole step
A half step	A whole step	A half step	A half step

Page 34, No. 6 (other options are possible)

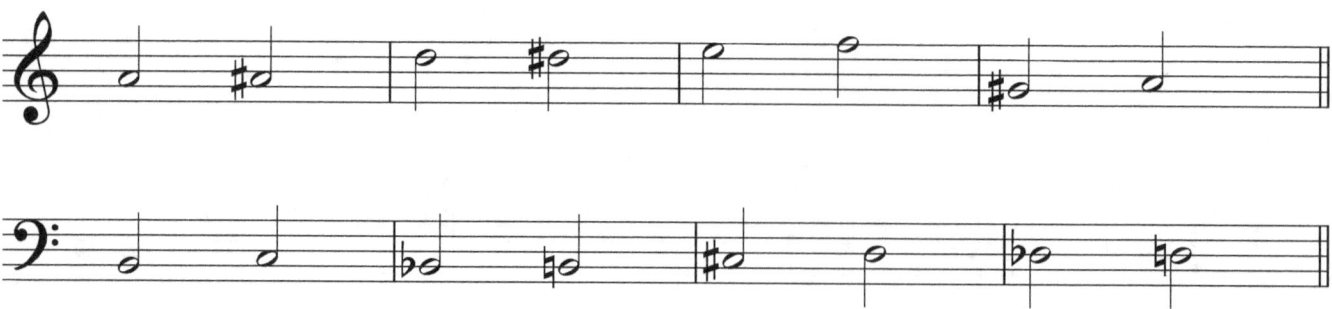

Page 35, No. 7 (other options are possible)

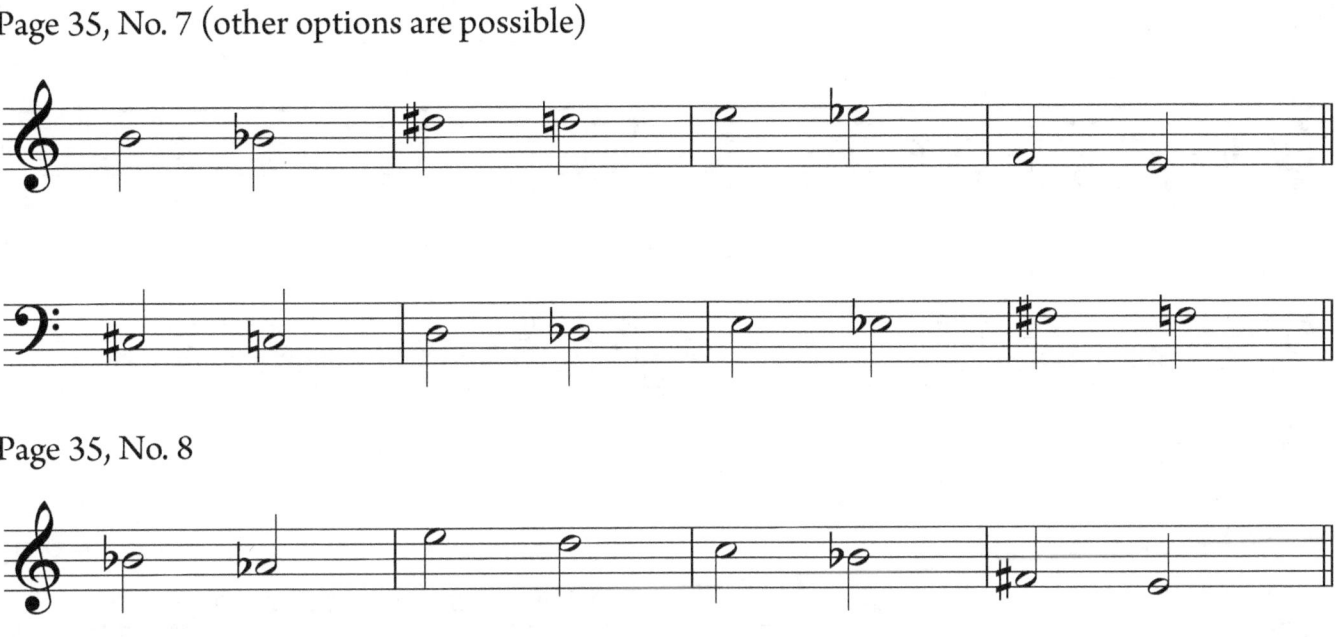

Page 35, No. 8

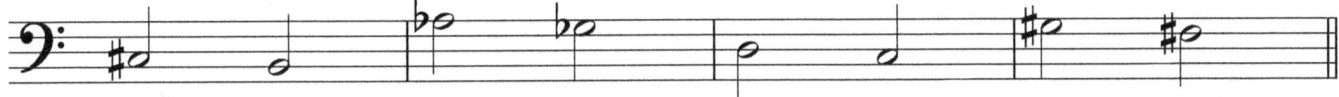

Page 35, No. 9

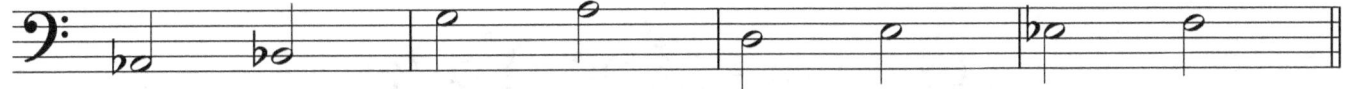

Page 36, No. 1

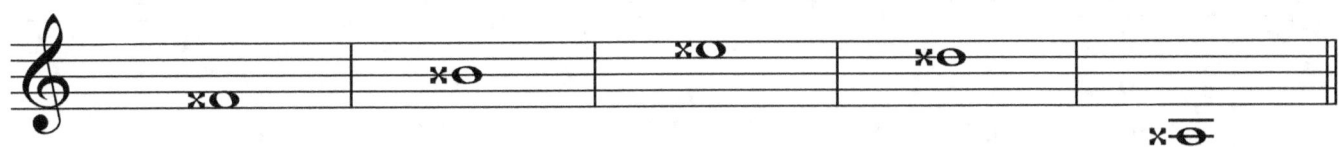

Page 37, No. 2

© San Marco Publications 2018

Page 38, No. 1

Page 39, No. 2

Jean Sibelius
Symphony No. 3, III

Wolfgang Amadeus Mozart
Piano Concerto K270

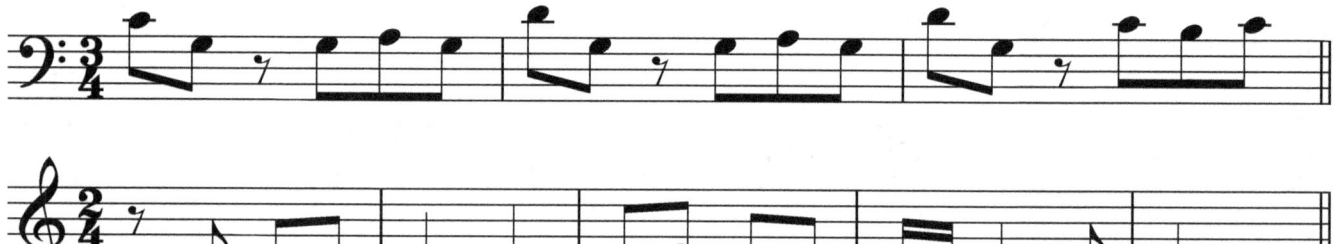

Lesson 4 - Major Scales

Page 41, No. 1

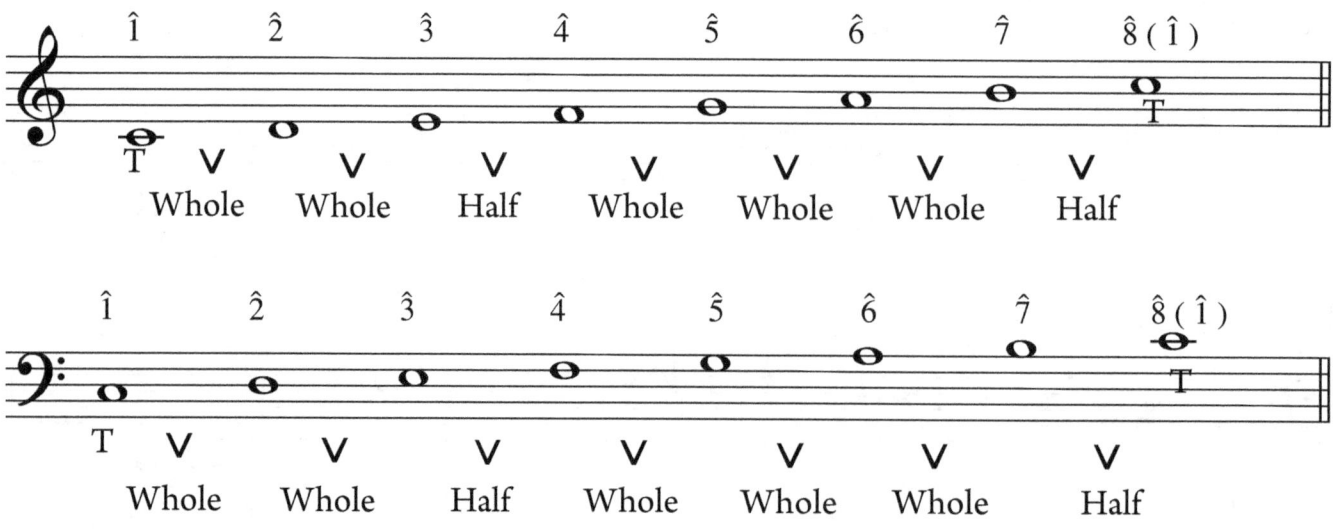

Page 42, No. 2

Page 42, No. 3

Page 43, No. 4

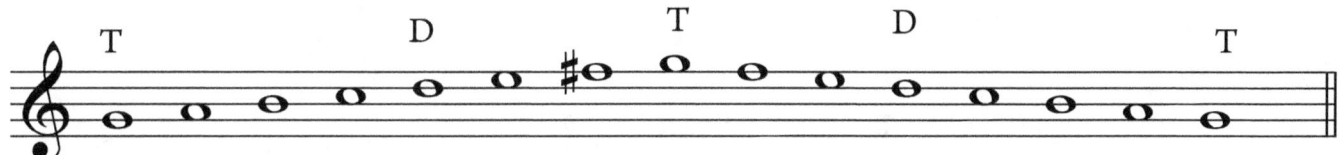

Page 44, No. 5

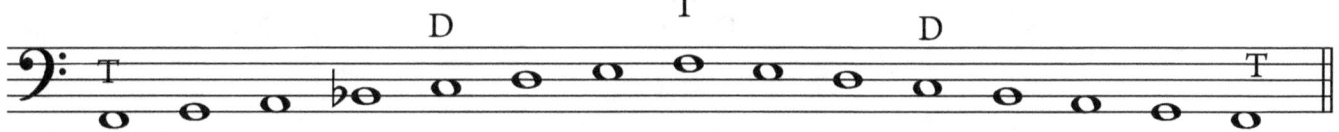

Page 45, No. 6

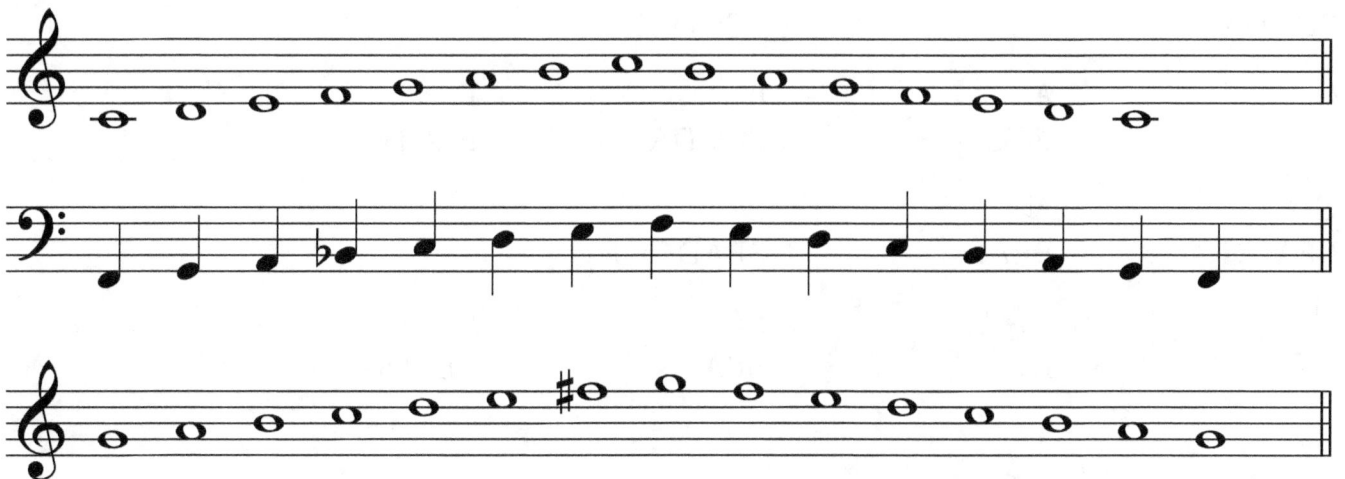

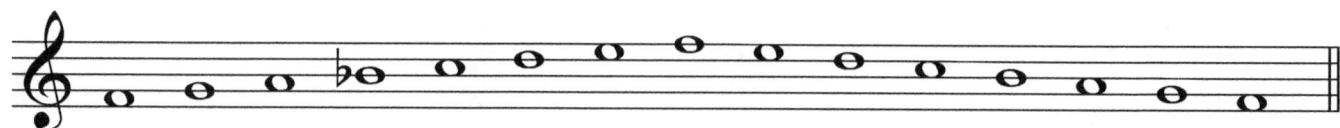

Page 46, No. 7

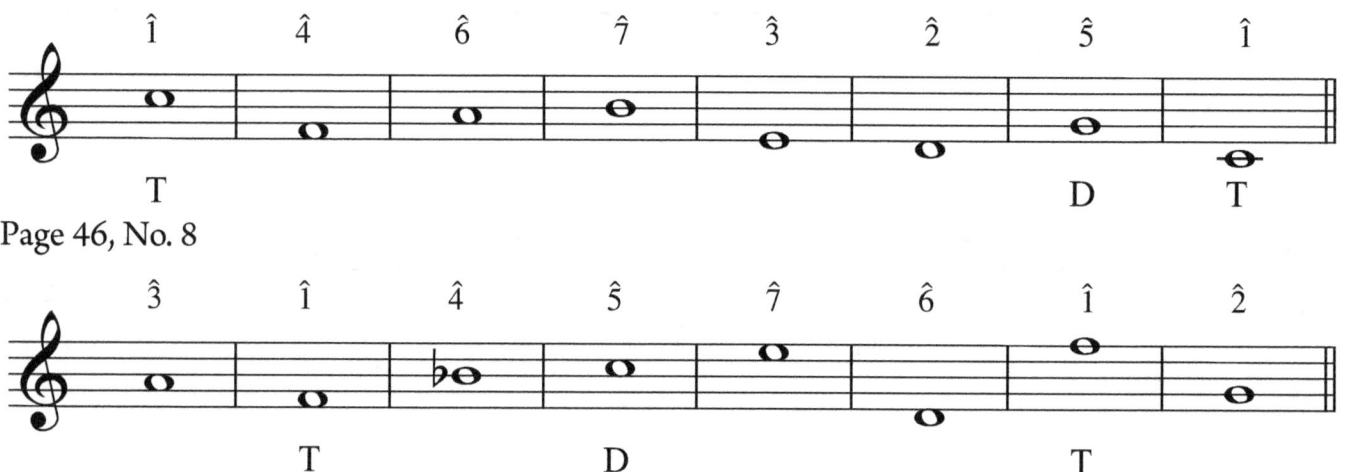

Page 51, No. 1

C#	D	F#	
FCGDAEB	FC	FCGDAE	

G	A	B	E
F	FCG	FCGDA	FCGD

G♭	A♭	C♭	
BEADGC	BEAD	BEADGCF	

B♭	F	E♭	D♭
BE	B	BEA	BEADG

Page 52, No. 1

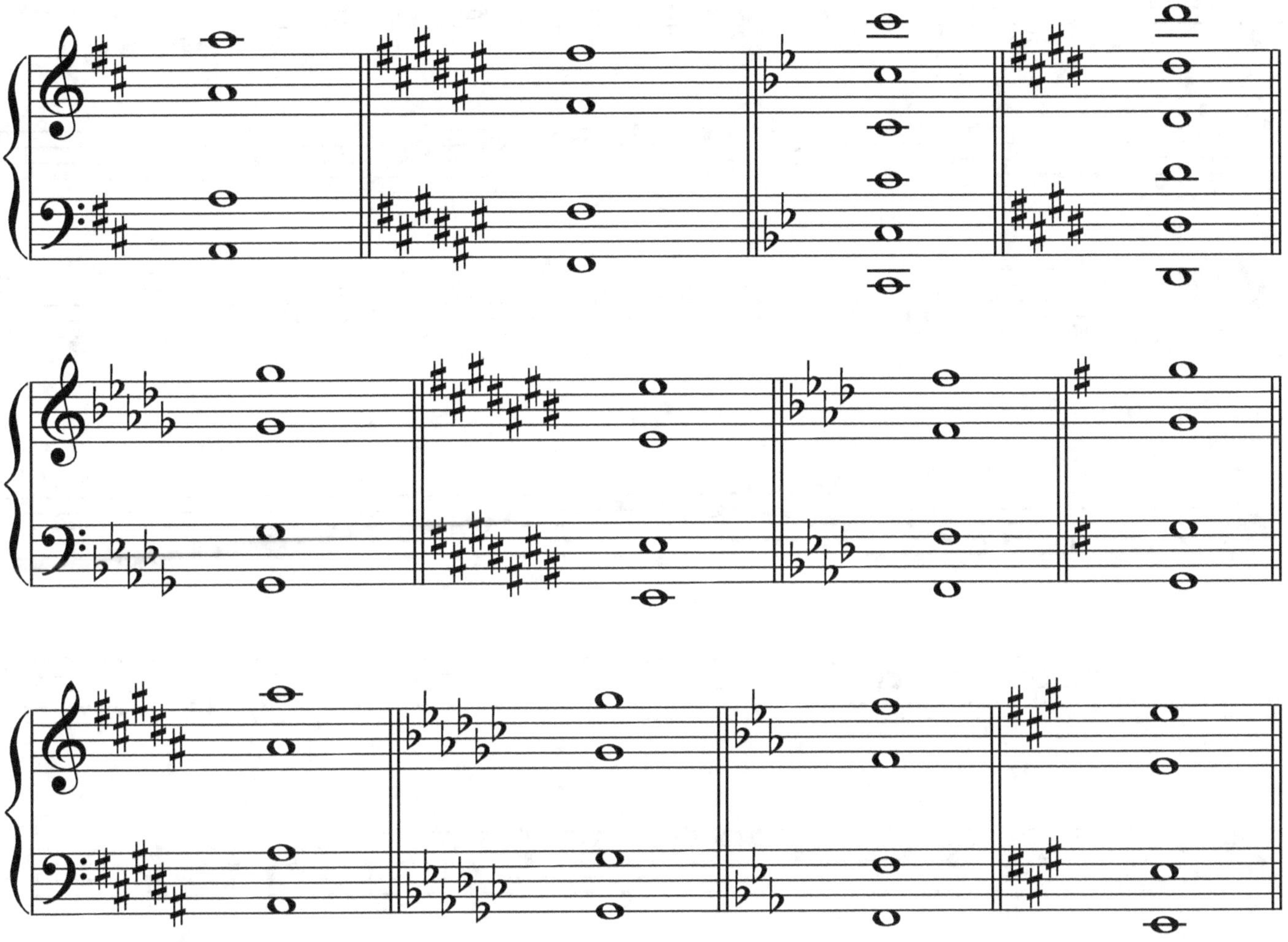

Page 53, No. 2

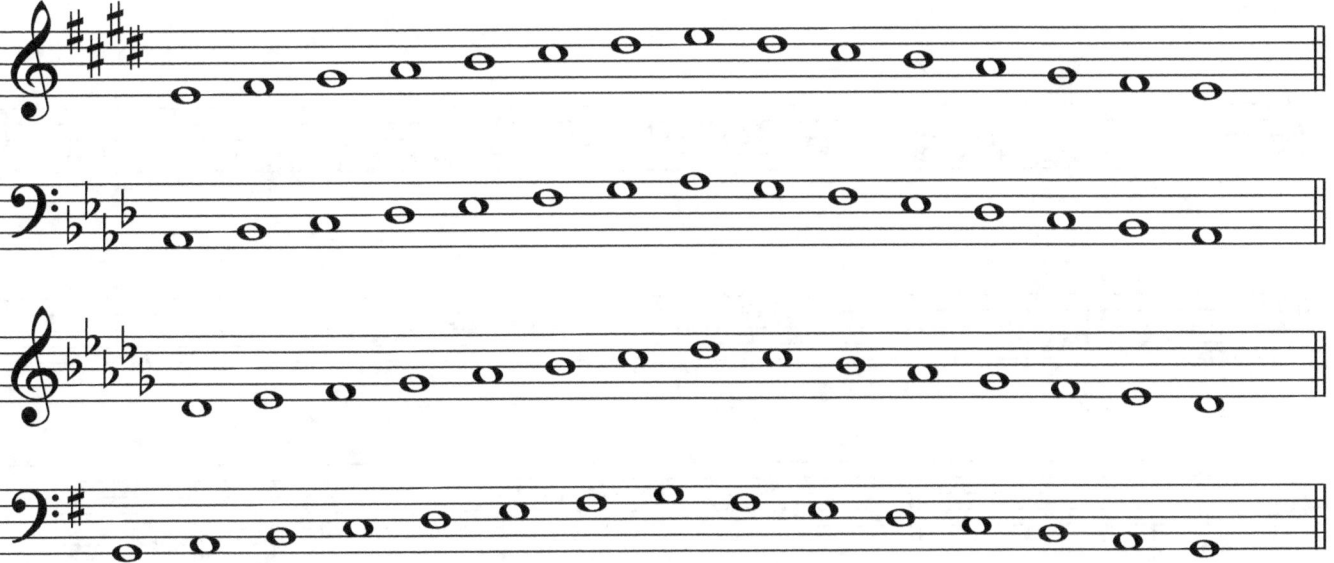

Page 54, No. 3

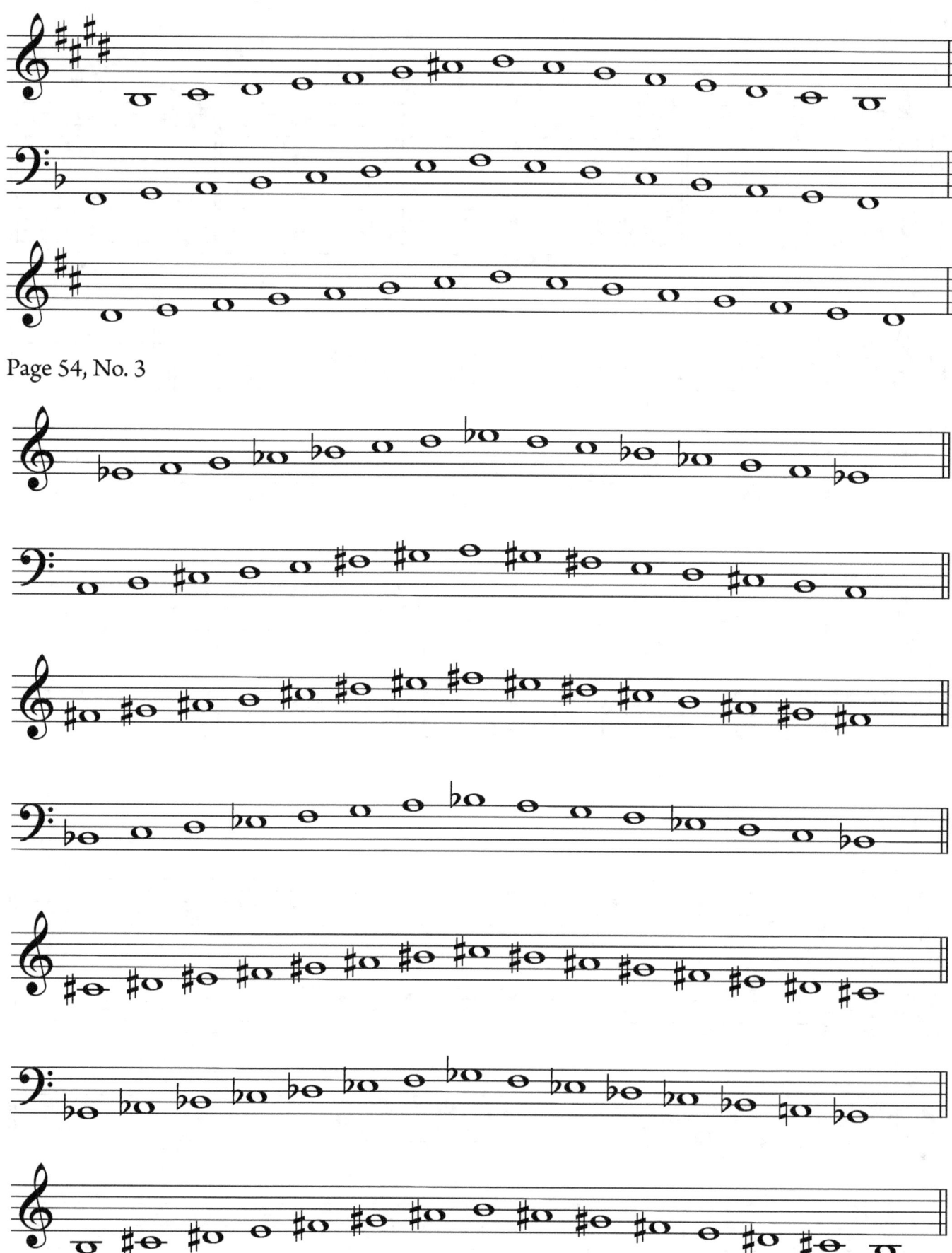

Page 55, No. 4

Lesson 5 - Minor Scales

Page 58, No. 1

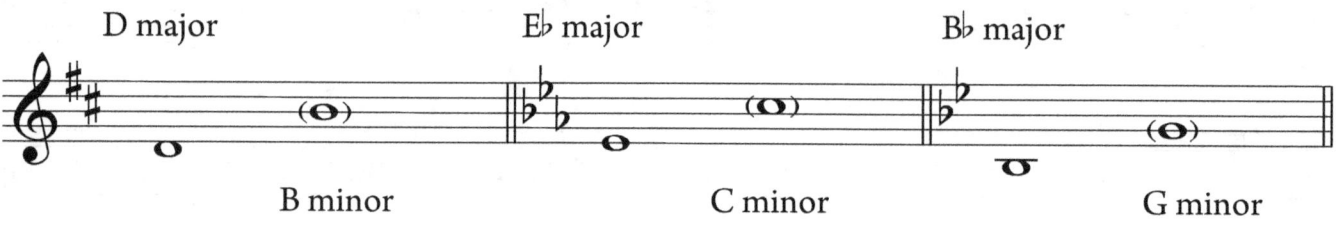

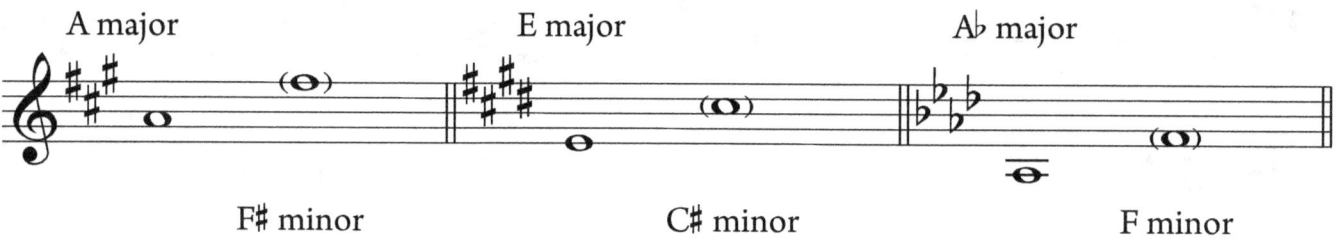

Page 59, No. 1

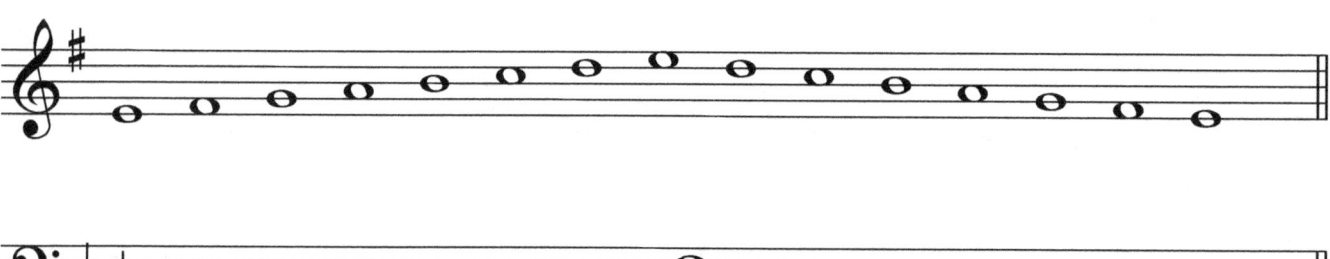

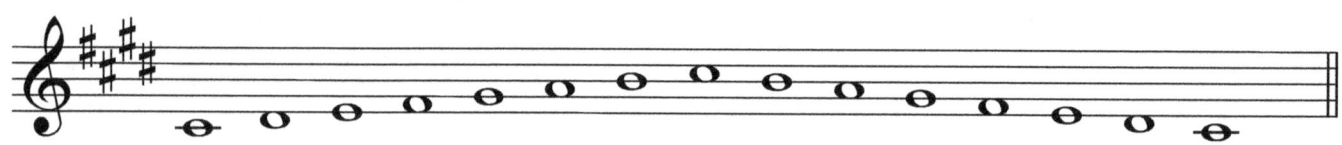

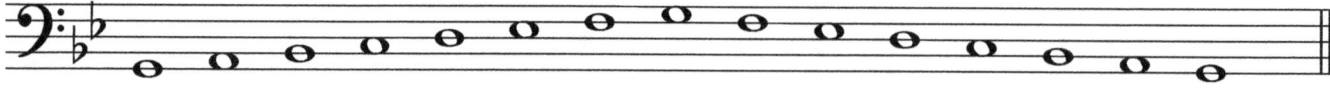

Page 60, No. 1

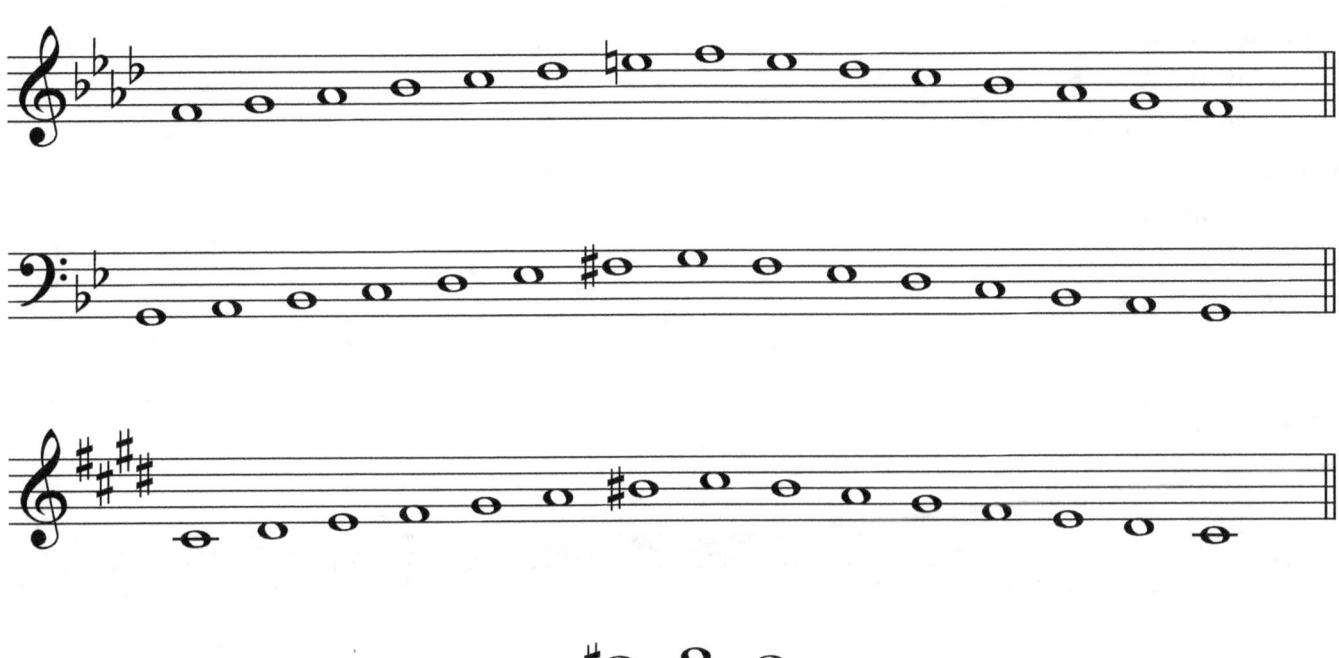

Page 61, No. 1

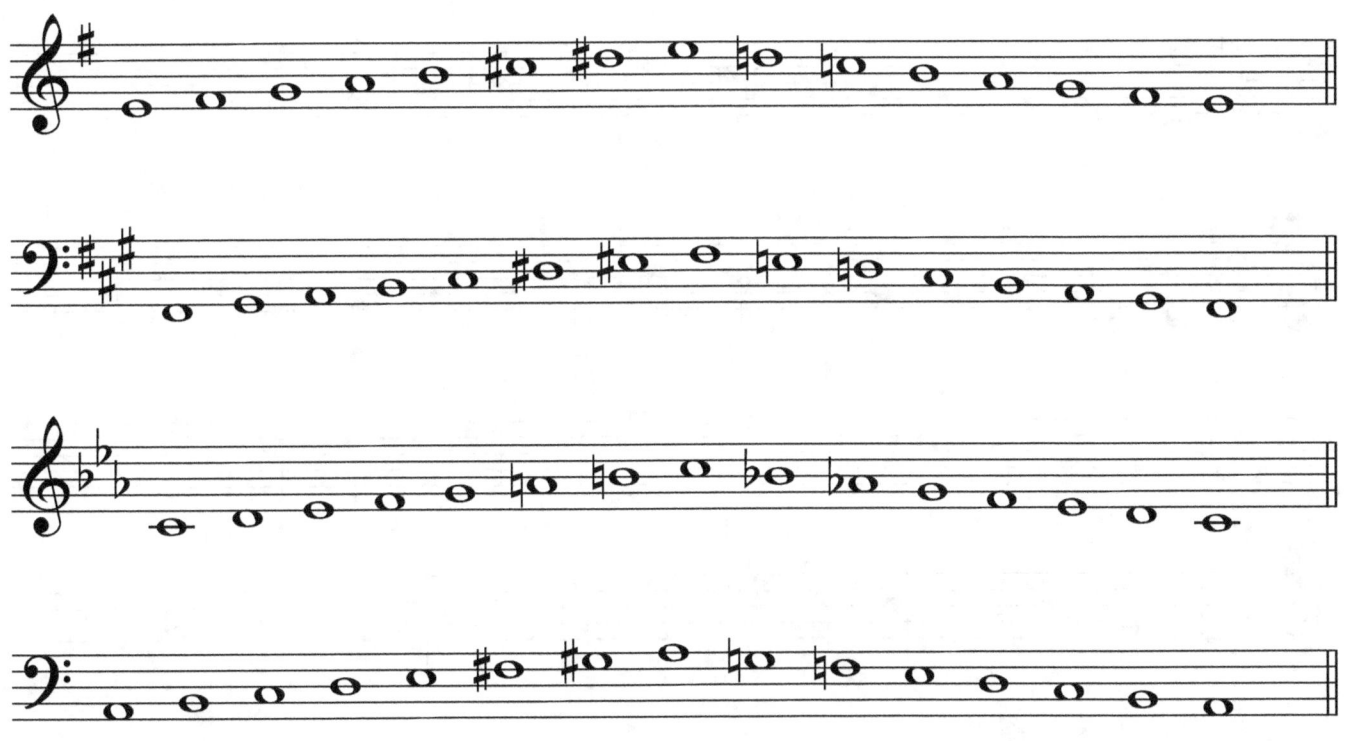

Page 63, No. 1

E natural minor
B♭ harmonic minor
G♯ harmonic minor
C melodic minor
D♯ harmonic minor
A melodic minor
G natural minor

Page 64, No. 2

Page 66, No. 1

a. The enharmonic tonic major of C♯ major is D♭ major.
b. The enharmonic tonic minor of B♭ major is A♯ minor.
c. The enharmonic tonic major of C♭ major is B major.
d. The parallel minor of D major is D minor.
e. The tonic major of G minor is G major.
f. The enharmonic tonic minor of E♭ major is E♭ minor.

Page 66, No. 1

G major

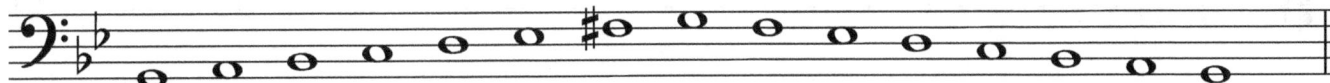

G harmonic minor

E melodic minor

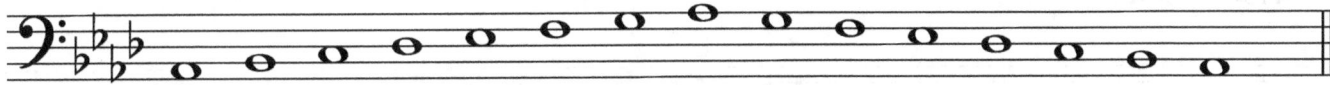

A♭ major

Page 67, No. 3

Page 68, No. 1

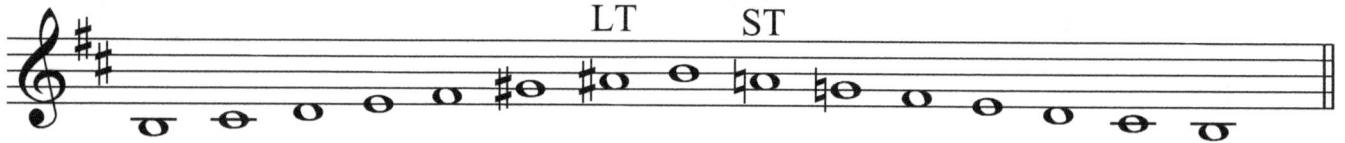

B melodic minor

G# harmonic minor

D# natural minor

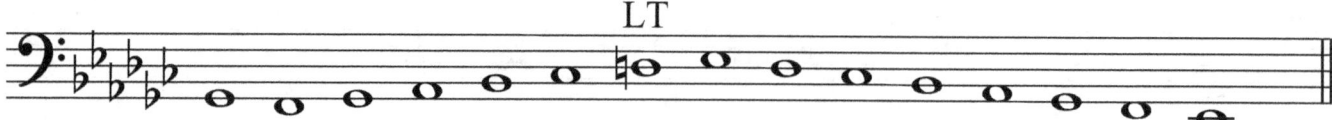

E♭ harmonic minor

© San Marco Publications 2018

Page 69, No. 2

E natural minor
B harmonic minor
C# harmonic minor
C melodic minor
F harmonic minor
A melodic minor
G natural minor

Page 70, No. 3

Page 71, No. 4

Page 73, No. 1

E♭ major
B♭ major
D minor
G minor
E minor
A♭ major
C minor

© San Marco Publications 2018

Lesson 6 - Other Scales

Page 75, No. 1

Page 78, No. 1

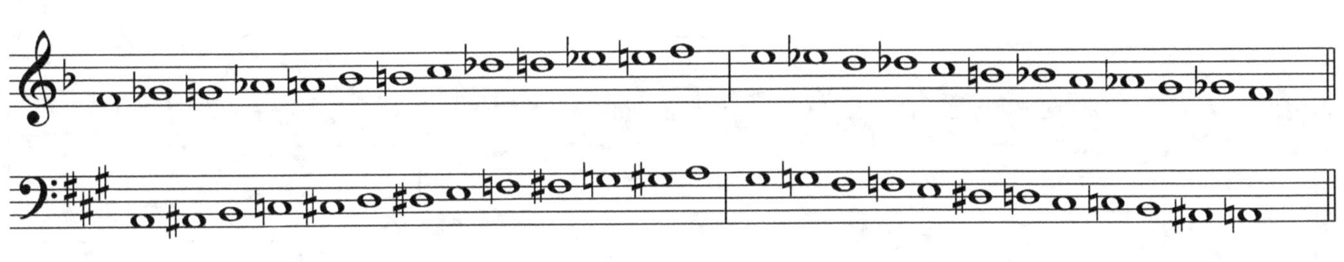

Page 79, No. 2

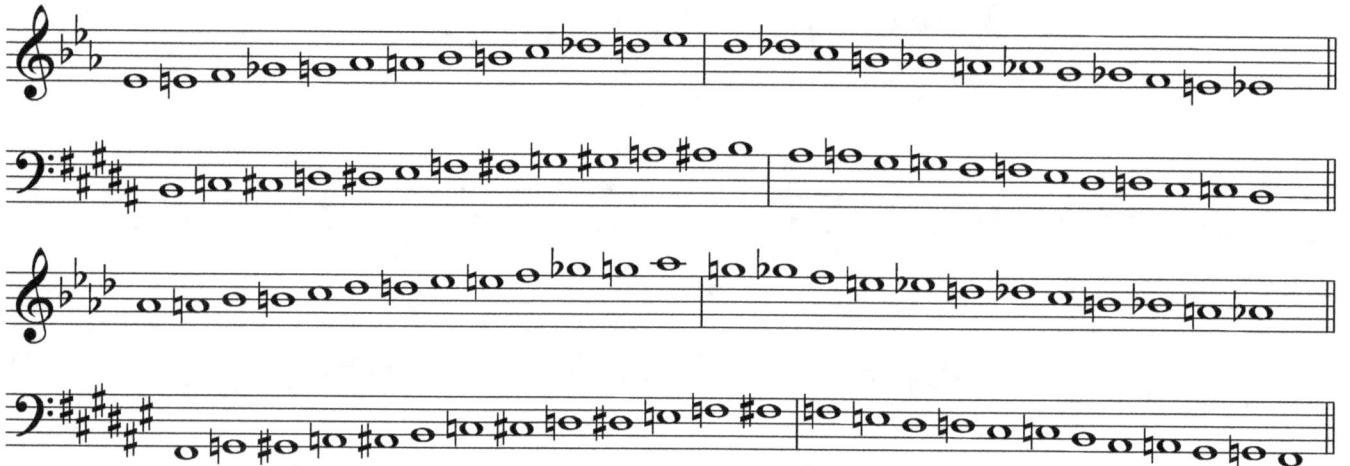

© San Marco Publications 2018

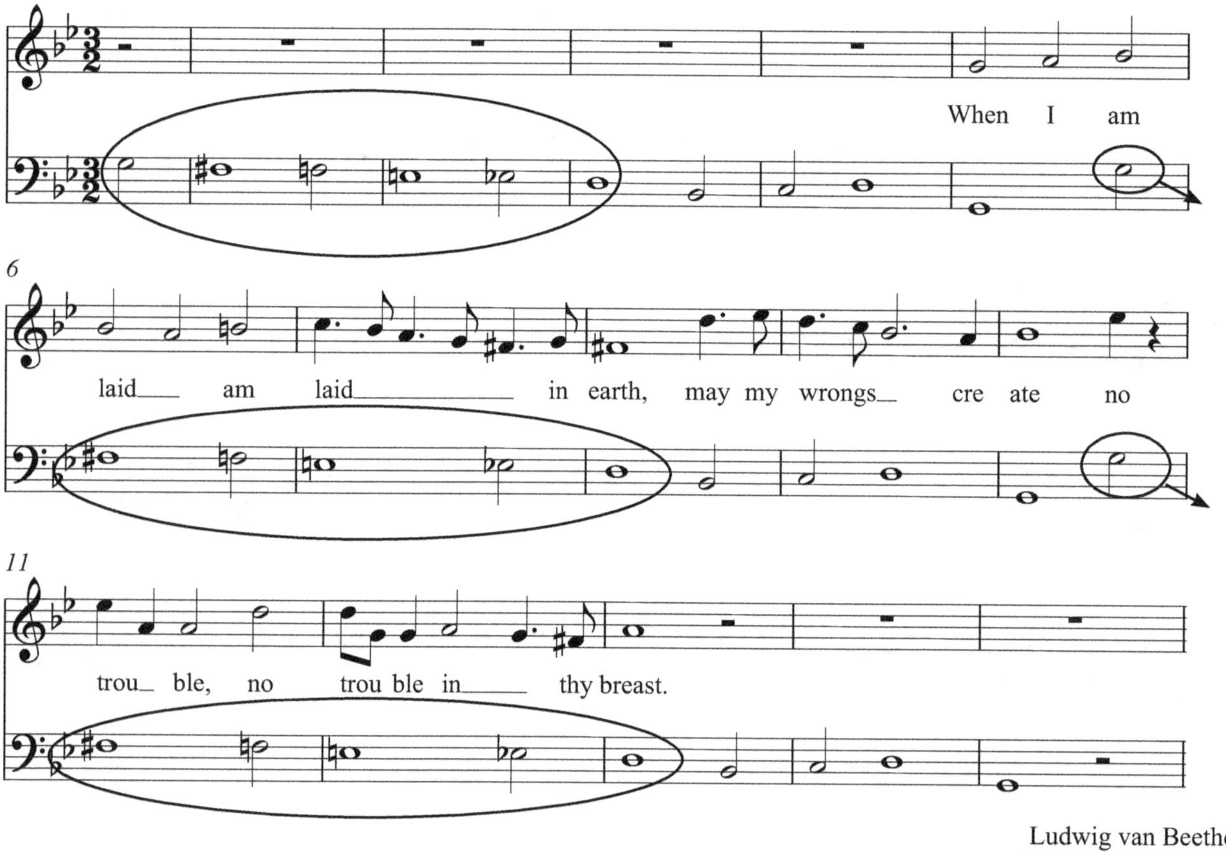

Page 81, No. 1

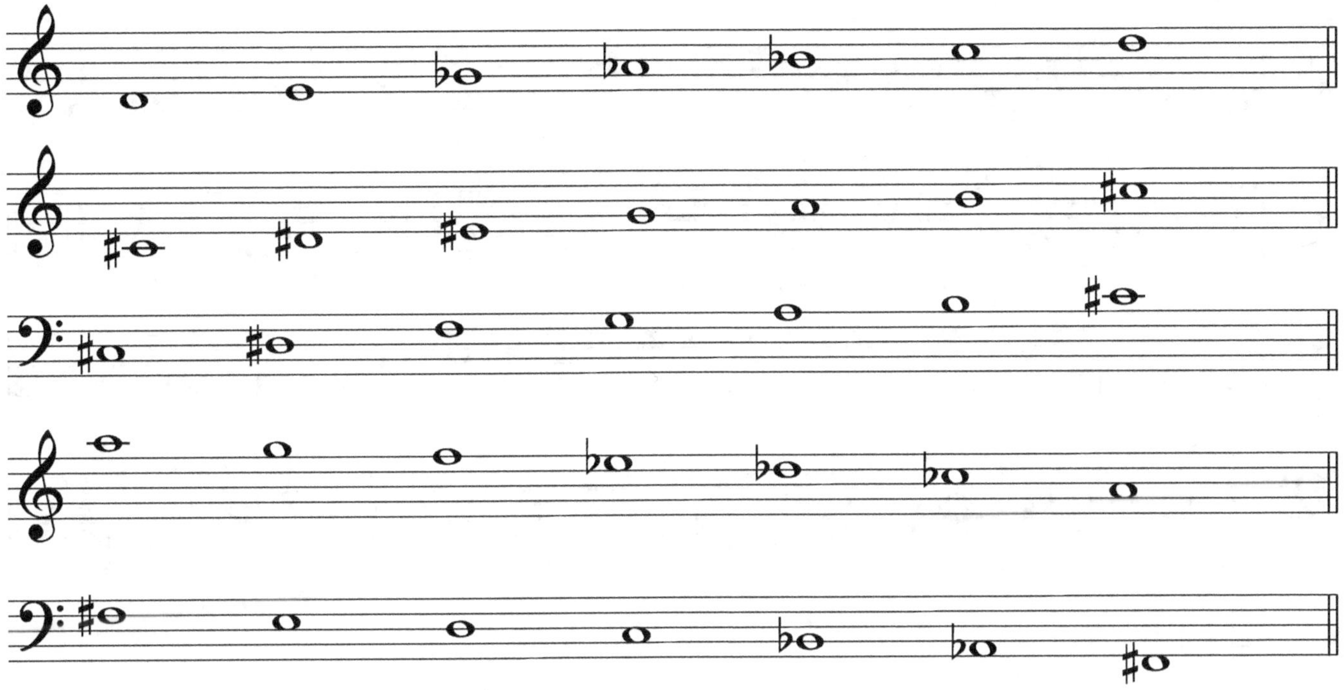

Page 81, No. 2 (other answers are possible)

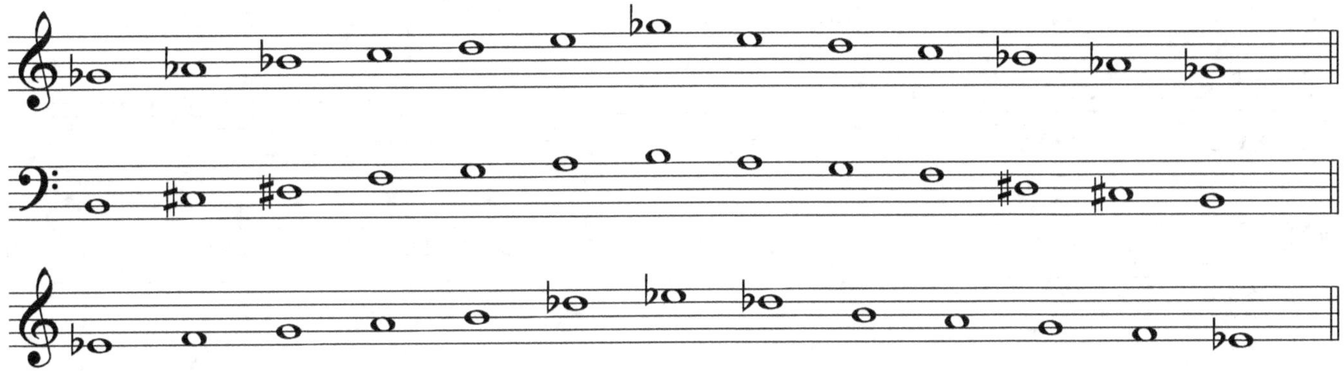

Page 83, No. 1 (other answers are possible)

Page 83, No. 2 (other answers are possible)

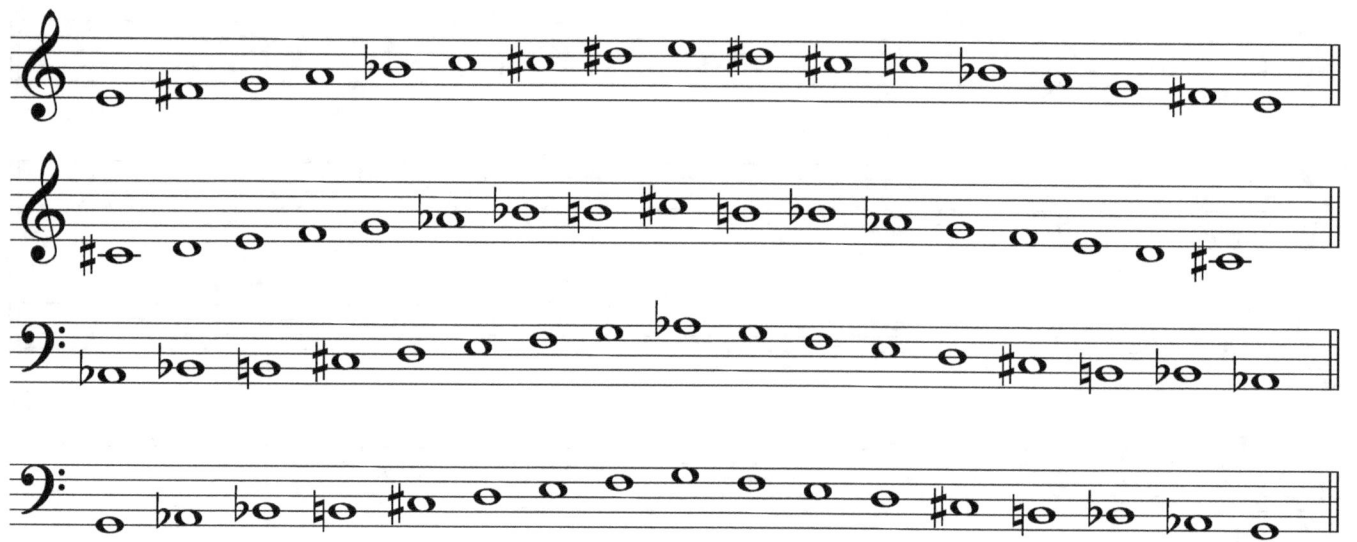

Page 84, No. 1

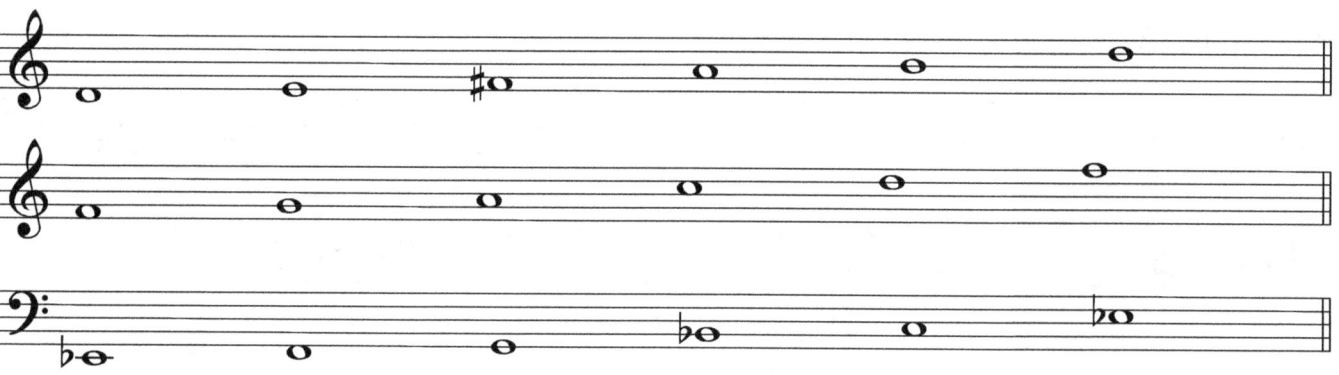

Page 85, No. 1

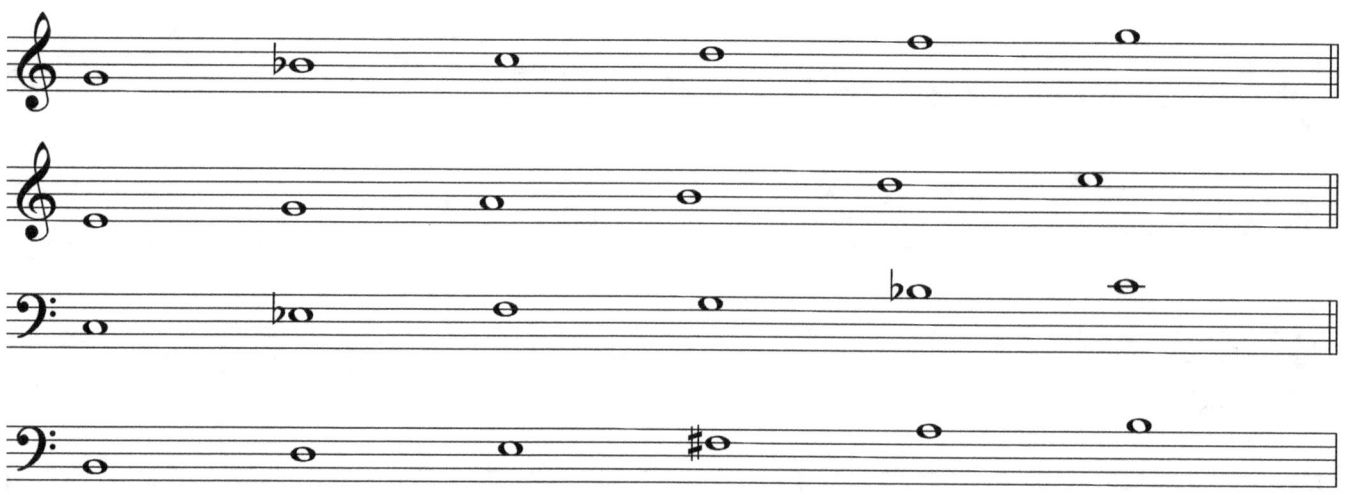

© San Marco Publications 2018

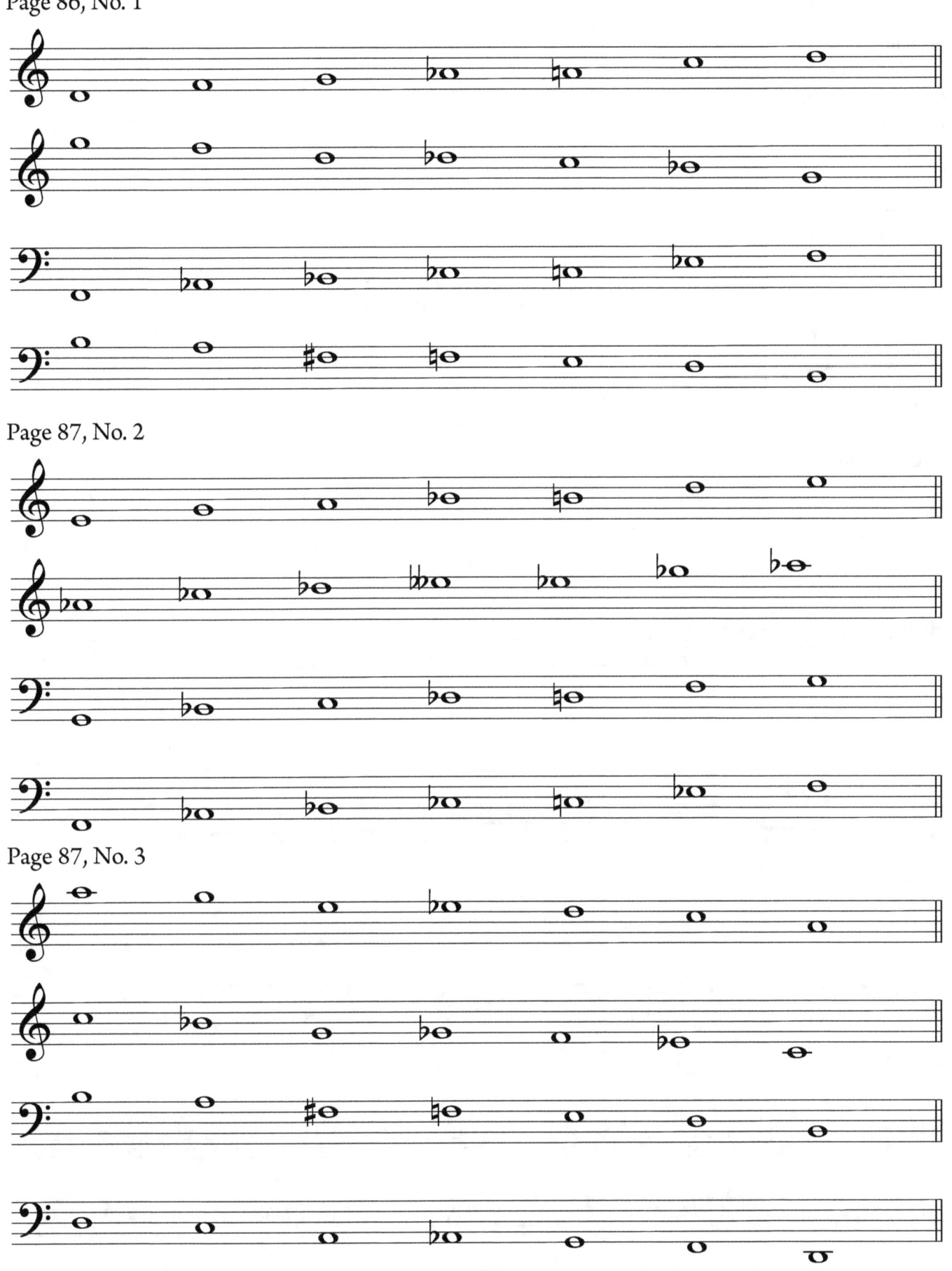

Page 88, No. 4

A♭ major
B melodic minor
E major pentatonic
C octatonic
D whole tone
F chromatic
D natural minor
A minor pentatonic

Lesson 7 - C Clefs

Page 91, No. 1

E A B F G C G F D
E B A E D D C G F

Page 91, No. 2

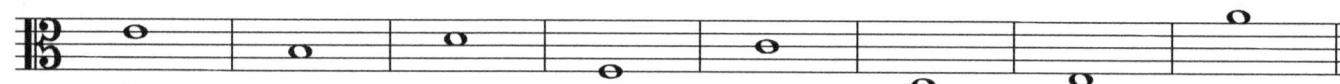

Page 91, No. 3

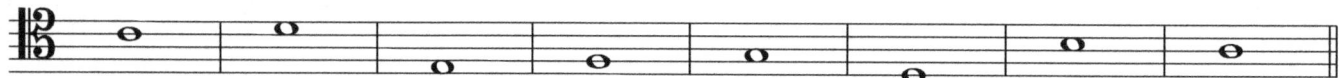

Page 92, No. 4

Wolfgang Amadeus Mozart
Cosi fan tutte

Page 92, No. 5

Gabriel Faure
Elegie, Op. 24

Page 93, No. 1

© San Marco Publications 2018

Page 93, No. 2

Page 94, No. 3

Page 95, No. 1

Page 96, No. 2

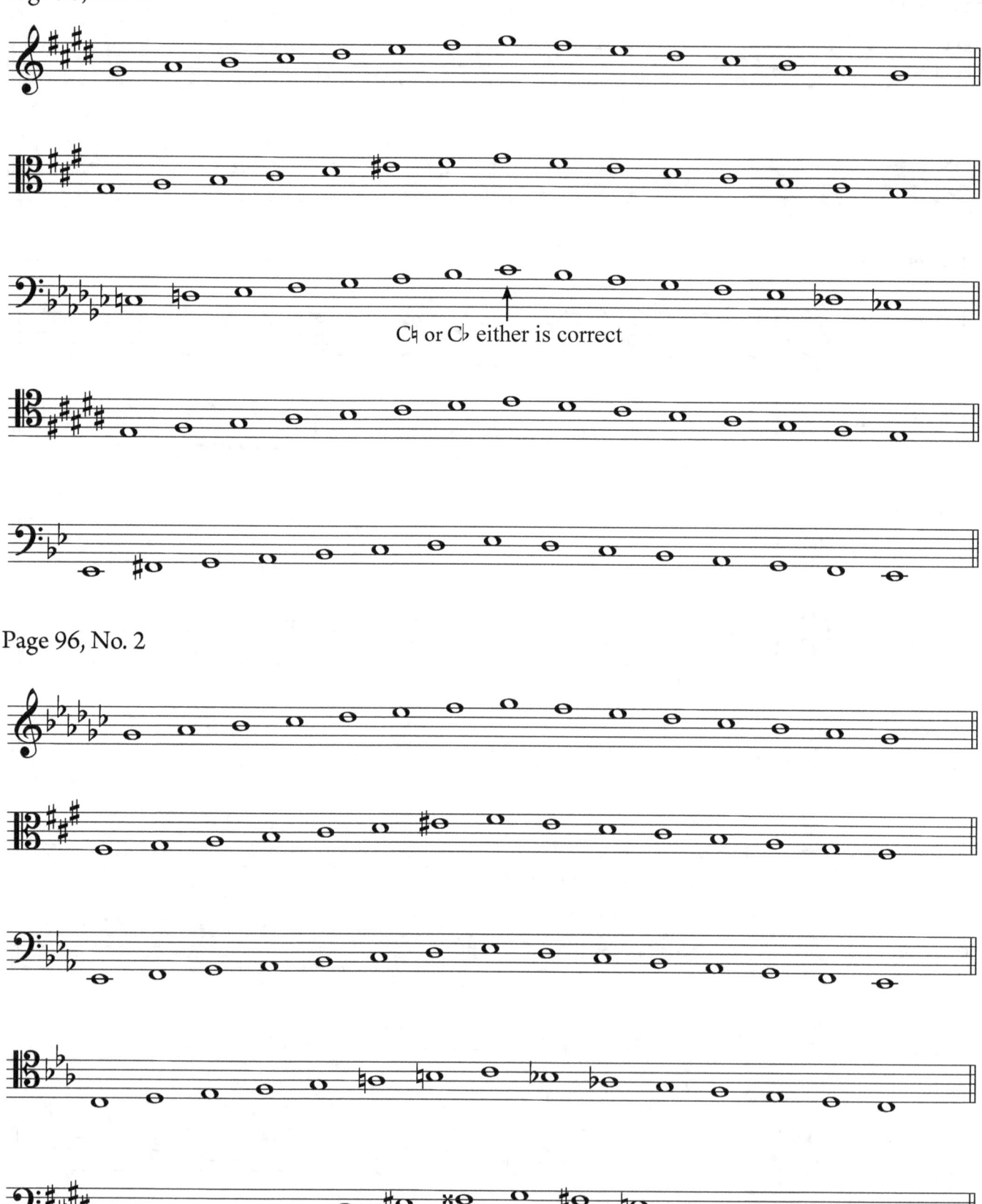

© San Marco Publications 2018

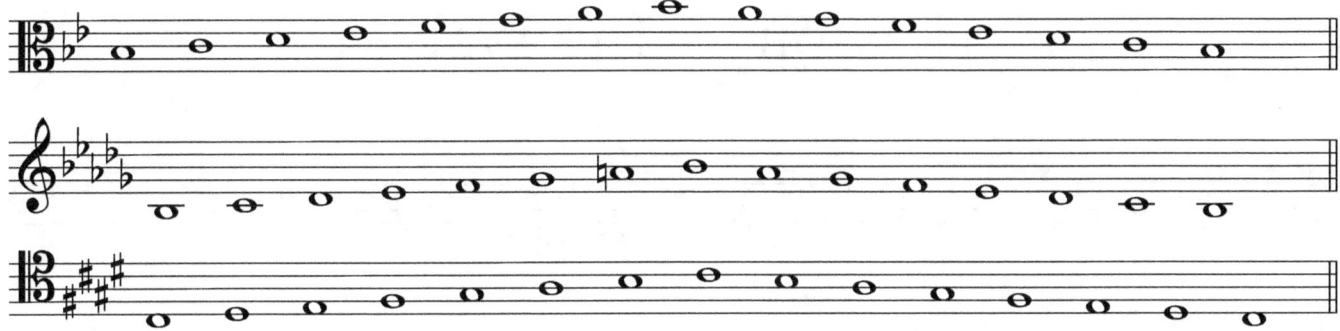

Lesson 8 - Modes

Page 101, No. 1

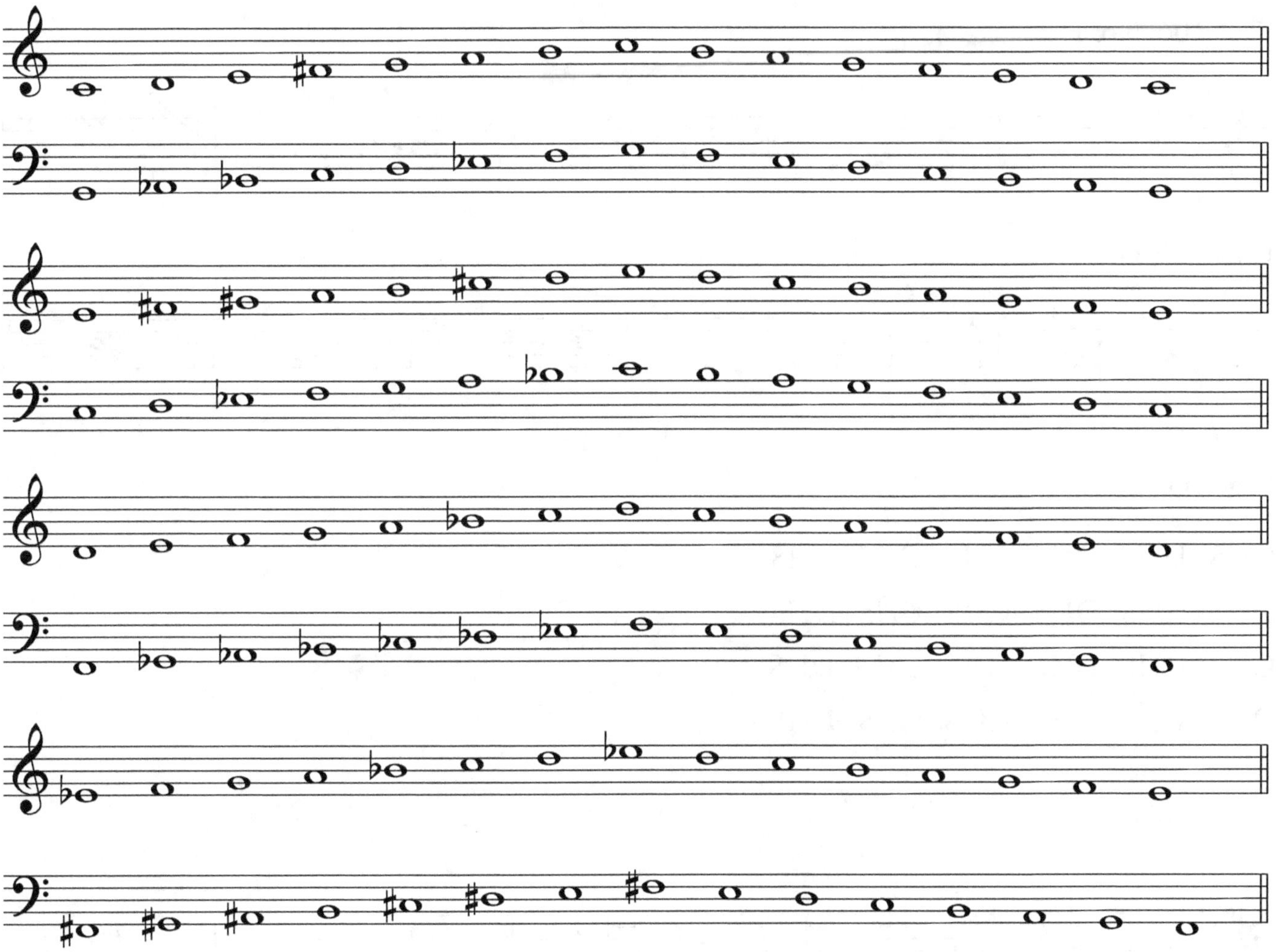

Page 102-103, No. 1

F dorian
G lydian
A locrian
E♭ mixolydian
G phrygian

B♭ mixolydian
D aeolian
F♯ dorian
B lydian

© San Marco Publications 2018

Lesson 9 - Intervals

Page 105, No. 1

Page 105, No. 2

Page 106, No. 1

Page 106, No. 2

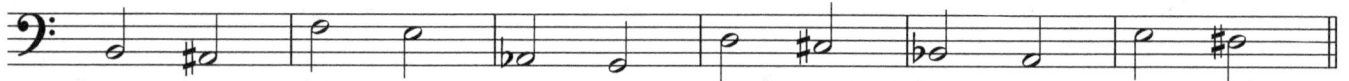

Page 106, No. 3

CHS DHS DHS CHS CHS DHS
DHS CHS DHS CHS CHS DHS
CHS DHS DHS CHS DHS DHS
DHS CHS CHS DHS CHS DHS

Page 107, No. 1

Page 107, No. 2

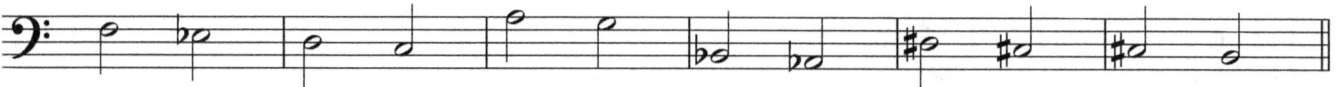

Page 108, No. 1

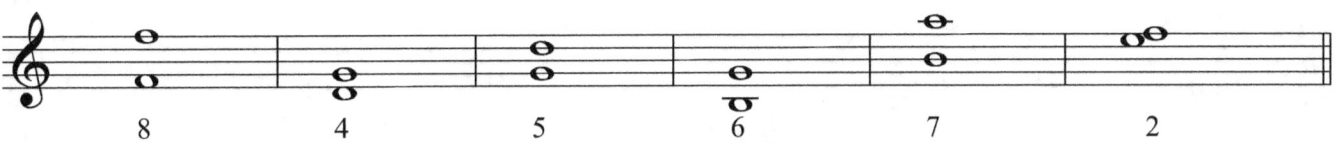

Page 109, No. 2

Page 109, No. 3

4 5 3 8 6 7 6 2

7 5 3 2 1 4 5 6

2 4 8 3 1 8 5 5

8 2 5 1 3 7 4 4

Page 110, No. 1

maj 2 maj 6 maj 7 maj 3 maj 7 maj 2 maj 6 maj 6

maj 2 maj 7 maj 3 maj 7 maj 6 maj 3 maj 7 maj 2

Page 111, No. 1

maj 6 per 4 maj 7 per 8 maj 2 per 4

maj 7 maj 3 per 4 per 5 per 8 per 1

© San Marco Publications 2018

Page 112, No. 1

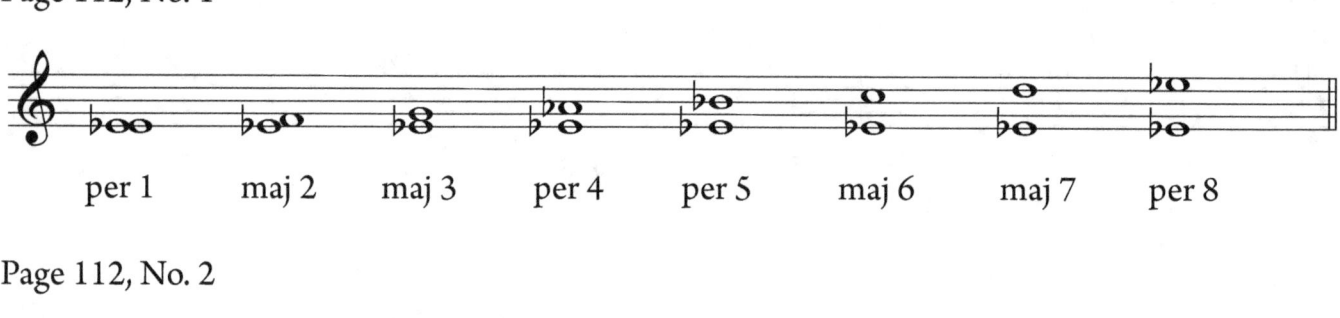

Page 112, No. 2

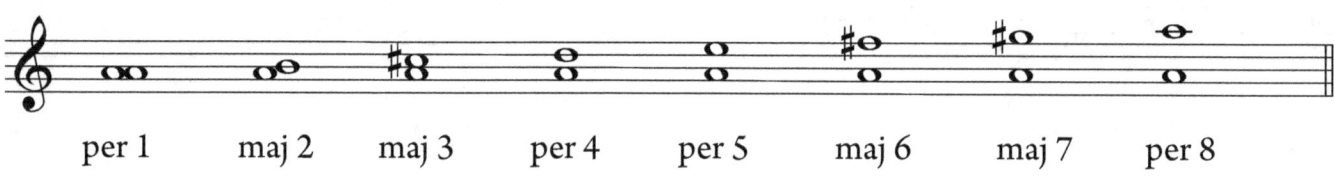

Page 112, No. 3

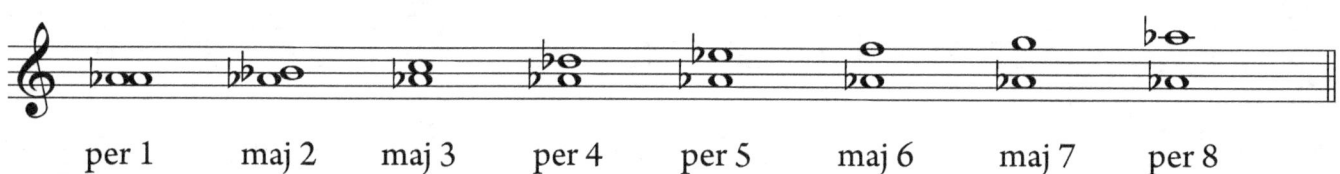

Page 113, No. 1

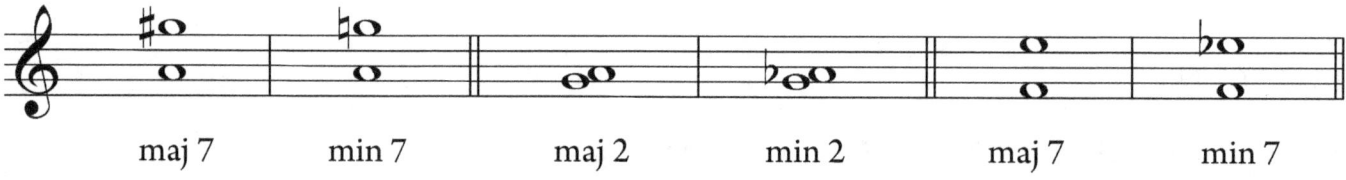

Page 114, No. 2

© San Marco Publications 2018

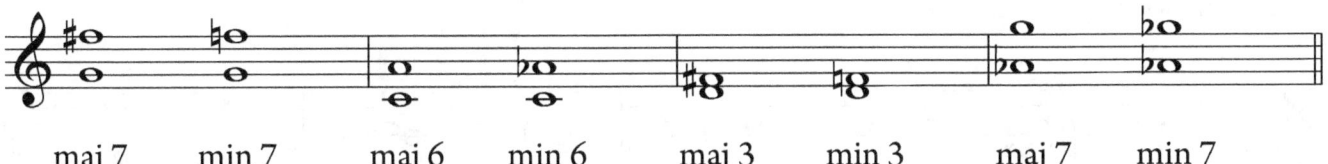

| maj 7 | min 7 | maj 6 | min 6 | maj 3 | min 3 | maj 7 | min 7 |

Page 114, No. 3

per 8   per 4   min 3   maj 2

per 5   per 4   maj 6   maj 3   min 2

Page 115, No. 4

per 5   min 3   per 4   maj 2   per 8   min 7   maj 7   per 5

per 5   min 6   per 5   min 6   min 7   maj 3   min 7   per 4

Page 115, No. 5

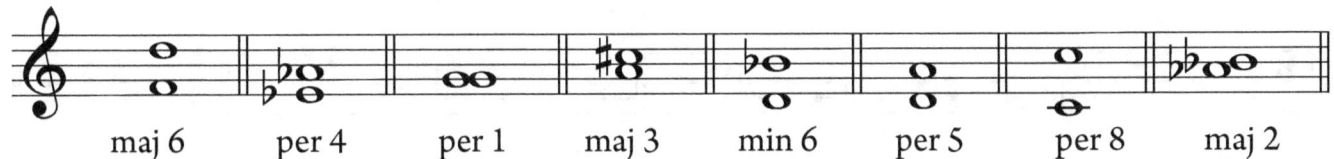

| maj 6 | per 4 | per 1 | maj 3 | min 6 | per 5 | per 8 | maj 2 |

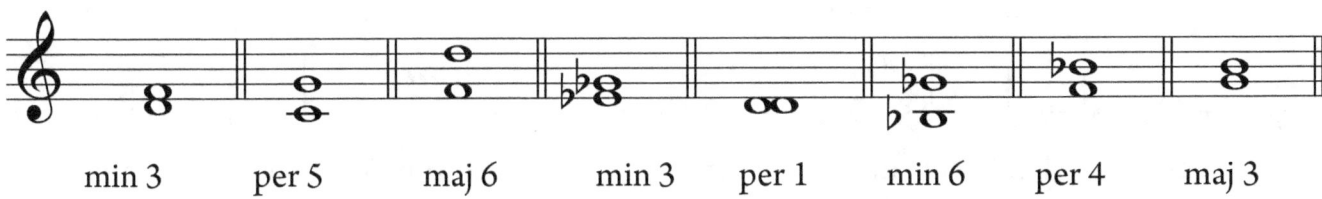

| min 3 | per 5 | maj 6 | min 3 | per 1 | min 6 | per 4 | maj 3 |

Page 116, No. 1

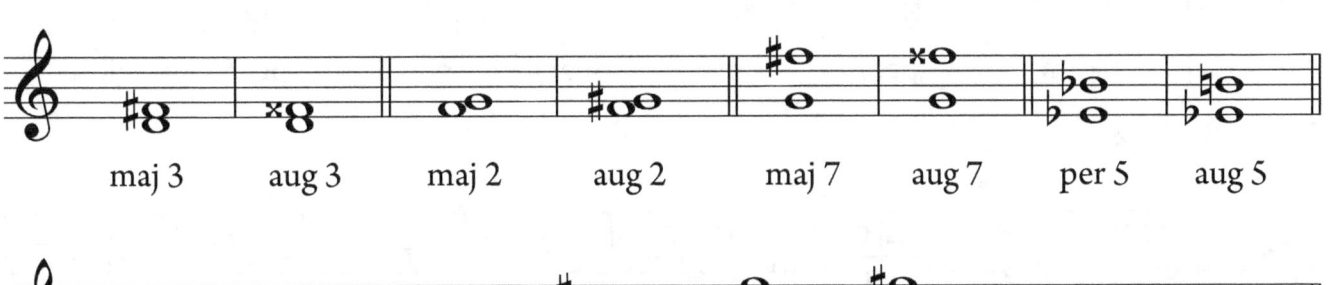

| maj 3 | aug 3 | maj 2 | aug 2 | maj 7 | aug 7 | per 5 | aug 5 |

| per 5 | aug 5 | per 8 | aug 8 | maj 6 | aug 6 | per 4 | aug 4 |

© San Marco Publications 2018

Page 117, No. 2

per 4 | aug 4 | maj 3 | aug 3 | maj 2 | aug 2 | per 8 | aug 8

maj 7 | aug 7 | maj 6 | aug 6 | per 5 | aug 5 | maj 3 | aug 3

Page 117, No. 3

Page 120, No. 1

per 5 | dim 5 | maj 6 | dim 6 | maj 2 | dim 3 | per 4 | dim 4

maj 7 | dim 7 | per 8 | dim 8 | per 4 | dim 4 | per 5 | dim 5

Page 120, No. 2

maj 6 | dim 7 | maj 7 | dim 7 | maj 3 | dim 3 | per 5 | dim 5

per 4 | dim 4 | maj 6 | dim 6 | per 5 | dim 5 | maj 7 | dim 7

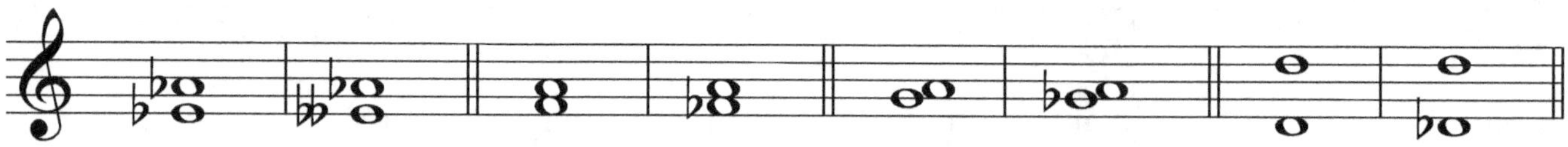

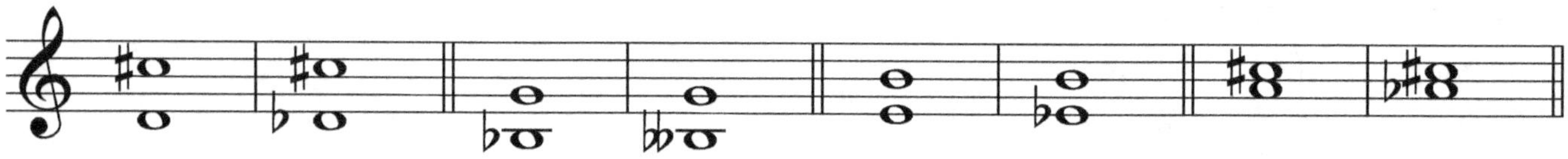

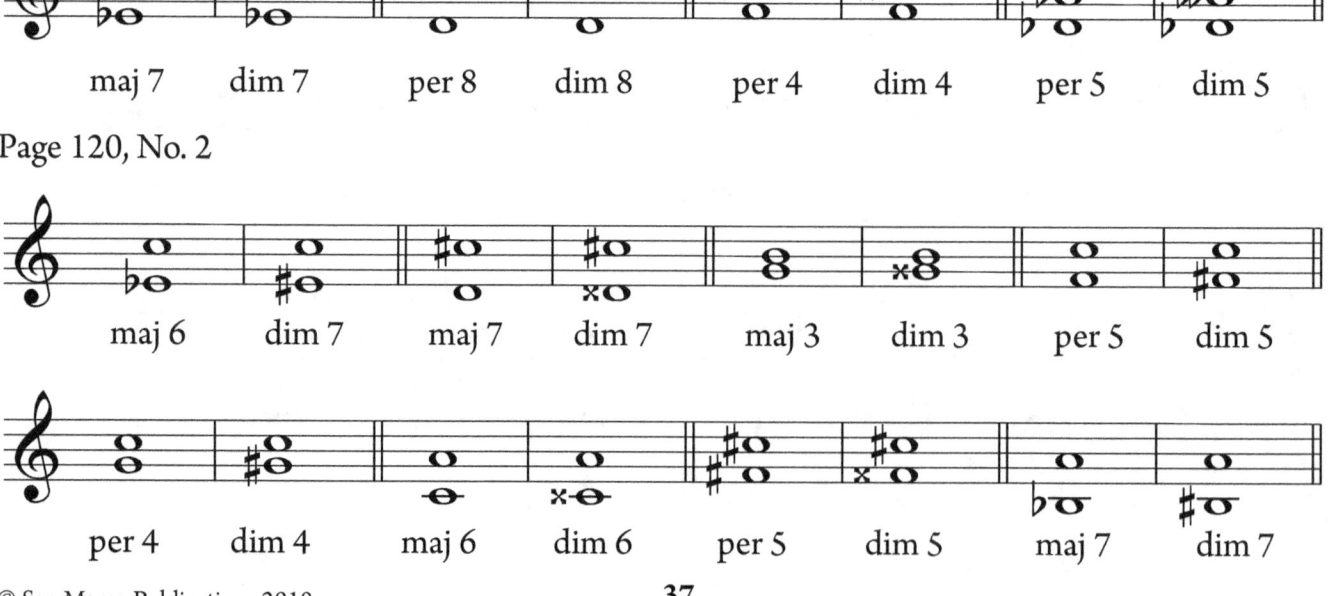

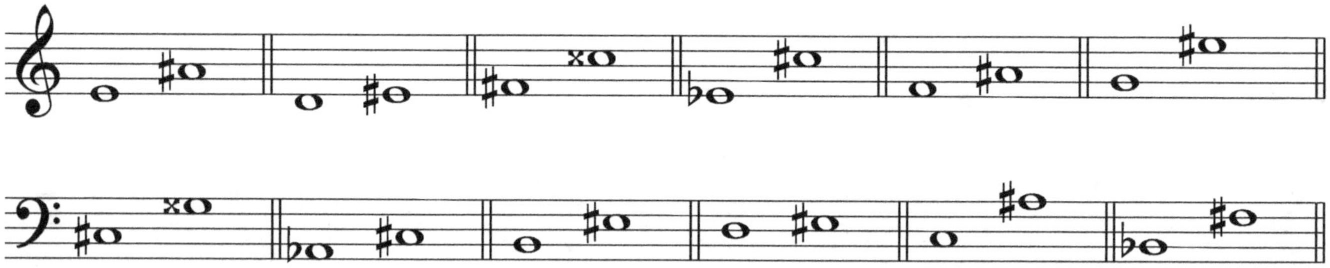

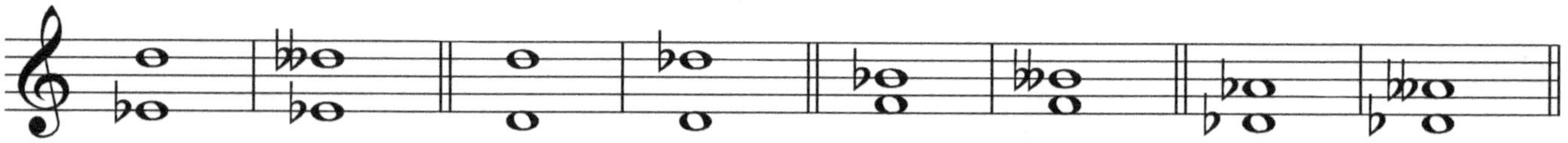

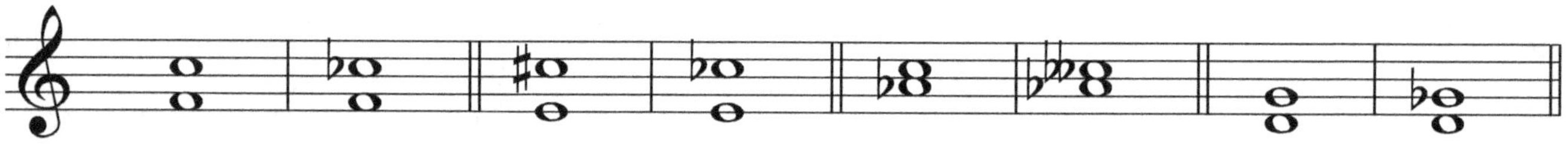

Page 120, No. 3

Page 121, No. 4

aug 5   min 6   per 5   maj 2   aug 3   aug 4
maj 3   per 8   dim 6   dim 5   dim 2   per 1

Page 121, No. 5

maj 2   dim 4   per 5   per 8   maj 3   min 2   min 3   maj 2

Page 121, No. 6

Page 123, No. 1

per 5   dim 3   maj 6   min 7   aug 2   dim 5

Page 123, No. 2

per 4   aug 5   aug 2   dim 7   dim 7   min 7

Page 123, No. 3

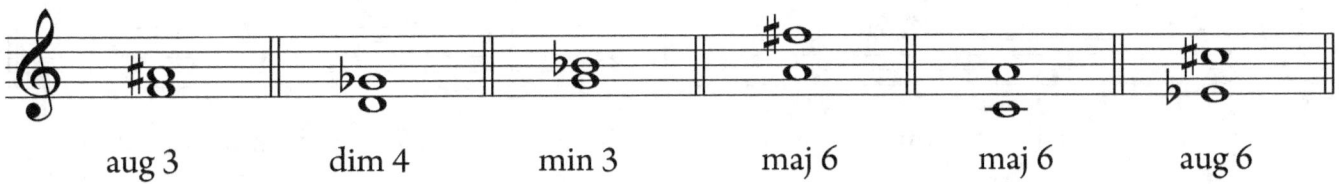

© San Marco Publications 2018

Page 123, No. 4

min 6   min 2   per 4   maj 3

per 4   per 4   min 3   min 3   per 4

per 4   per 4   min 2   maj 2   min 3

maj 2   dim 5   min 2   min 3   per 4

Page 124, No. 1

Page 126, No. 1

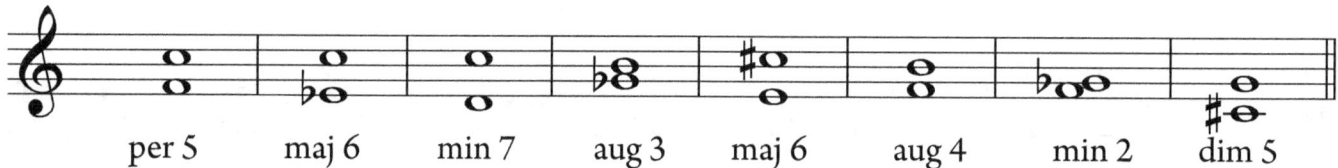

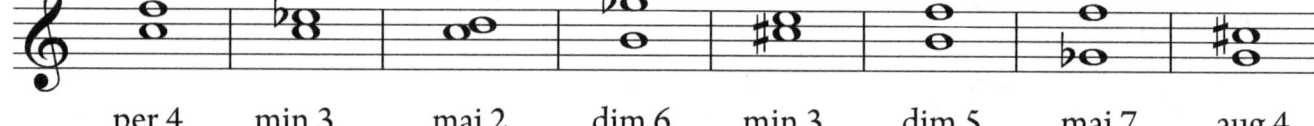

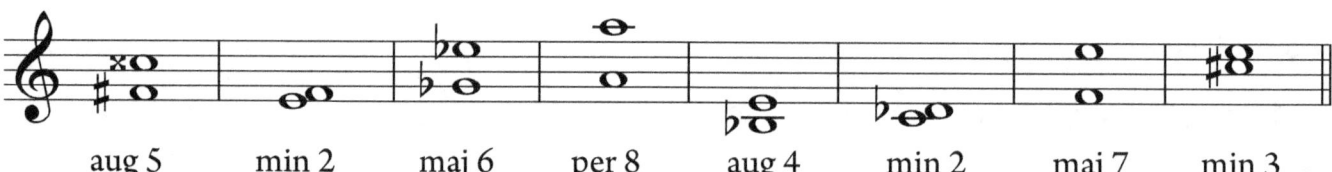

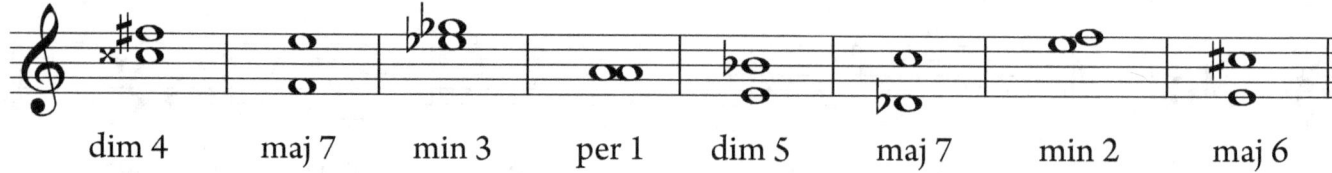

Page 126, No. 2

dim 6   min 3   per 6   dim 4   aug 1   min 7   aug 8   min 6
maj 2   maj 7   maj 3   aug 8   dim 8   min 3   dim 4   min 7

Page 127, No. 3

Page 128, No. 1

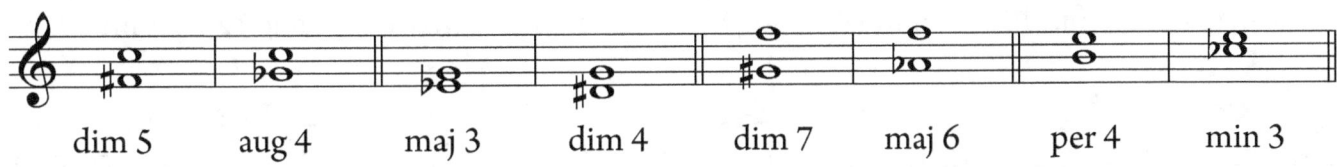

Page 128, No. 2

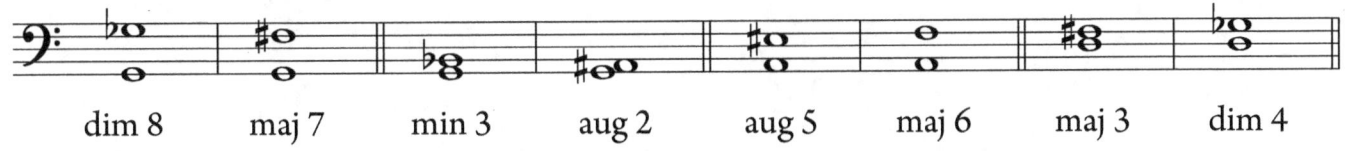

Page 129, No. 3

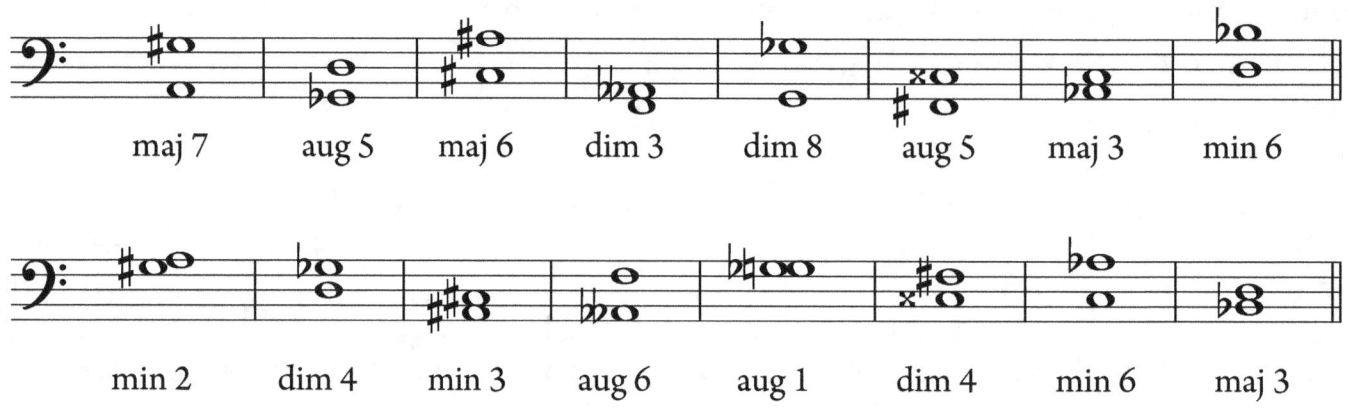

Page 130, No. 1

Page 131, No. 2

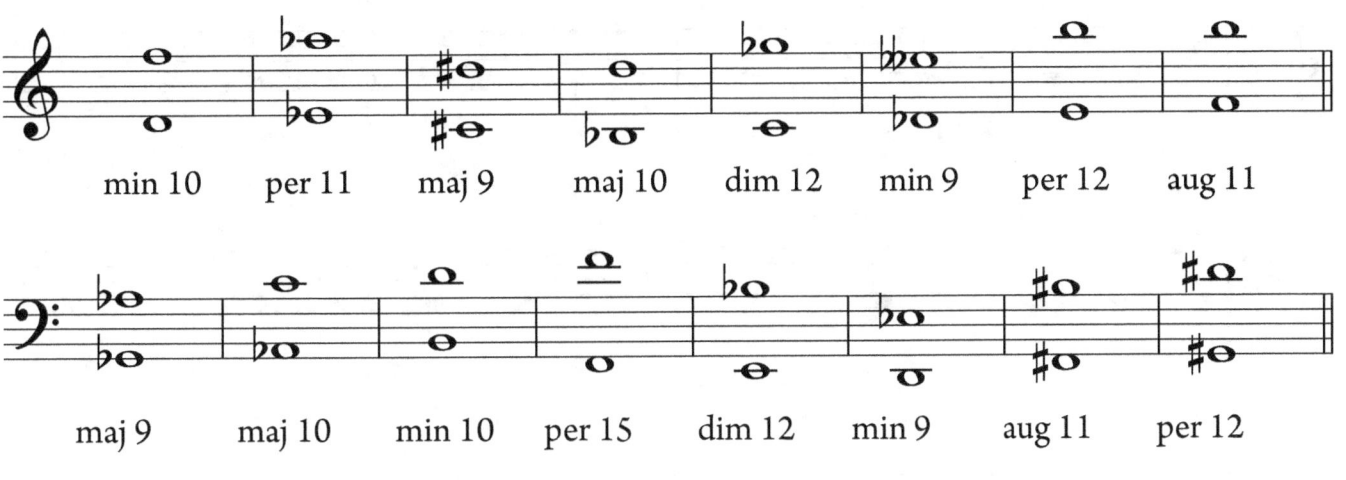

Page 131, No. 3

1. min 7   2. dim 12   3. min 10   4. per 12   5. min 3

Page 131, No. 4

1. per 12   2. maj 13   3. min 14   4. min 10   5. min 13   6. maj 6   7. maj 13

Lesson 10 - Meter 1

Page 134, No. 1

Page 135, No. 1

Page 136, No. 2

2/4, 4/4, 2/4, 4/4, 3/4

Page 136, No. 3

Page 137, No. 4

Page 137, No. 5

Page 139, No. 1

Page 141, No. 1

Page 142, No. 2

Page 143, No. 1

Page 143, No. 2

Page 145, No. 1

Page 145, No. 2

Page 146, No. 1

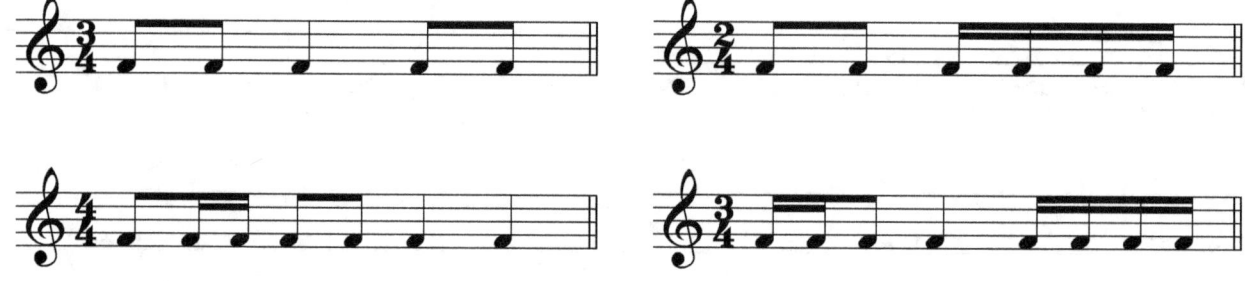

Page 147, No. 1

Page 148, No. 2

a) 4   b) 2   c) 2   d) 4   e) 2

Page 148, No. 3

Page 149, No. 4

3/4   3/4
2/4   2/4
4/4   4/4
3/4   4/4
2/4   3/4

Page 149, No. 5

Page 151, No. 1

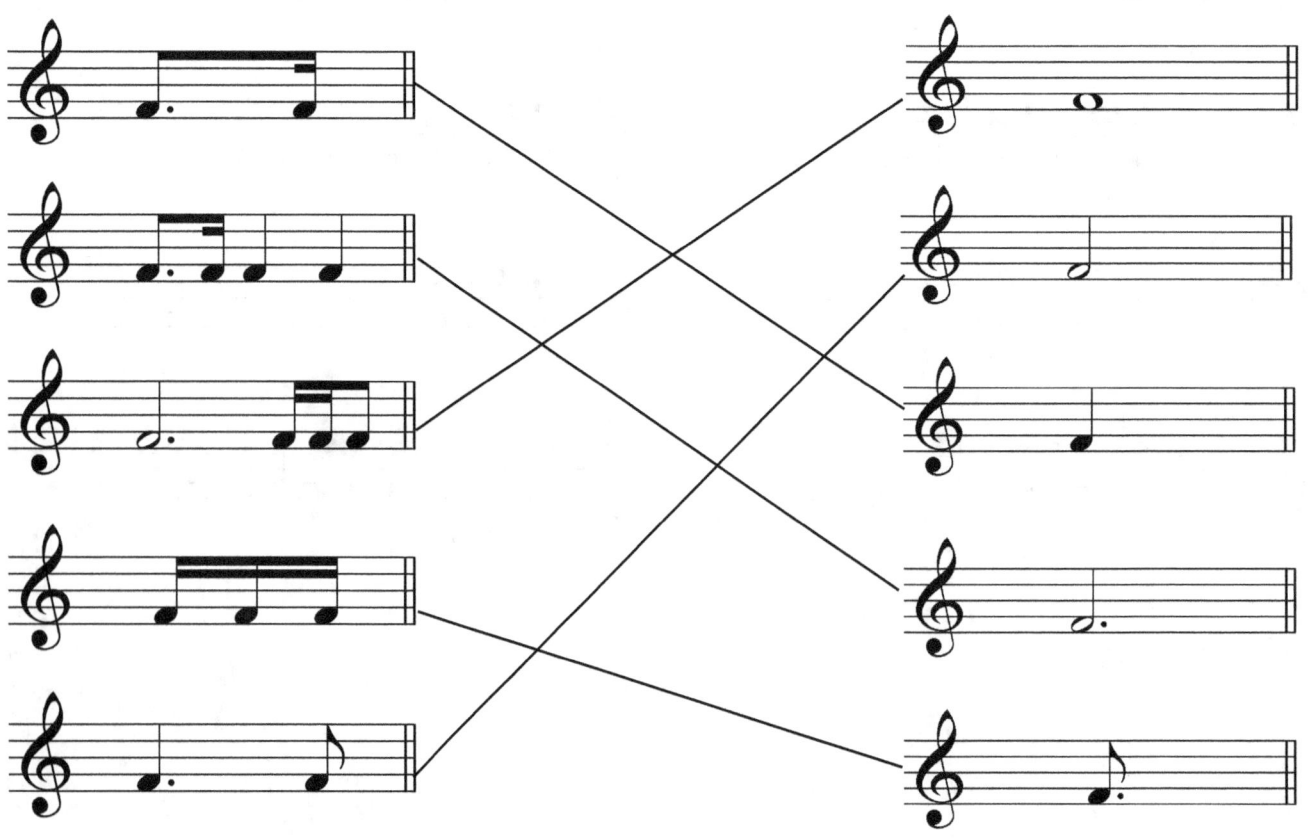

Page 152, No. 2

Bach
English Suite No.2

Corelli
Concerto Grosso
Op. 6, No. 11

Mozart
Sonata in G

Liszt
Hungarian Rhapsody No. 14

Tchaikovsky
Swan Lake

Mozart
Trio in C

Bach
Brandenberg Concerto No. 2

© San Marco Publications 2018

Page 154, No. 1

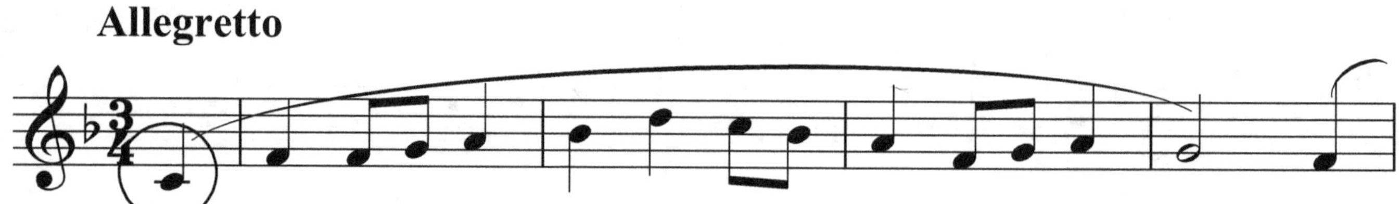
Allegretto

key: F major

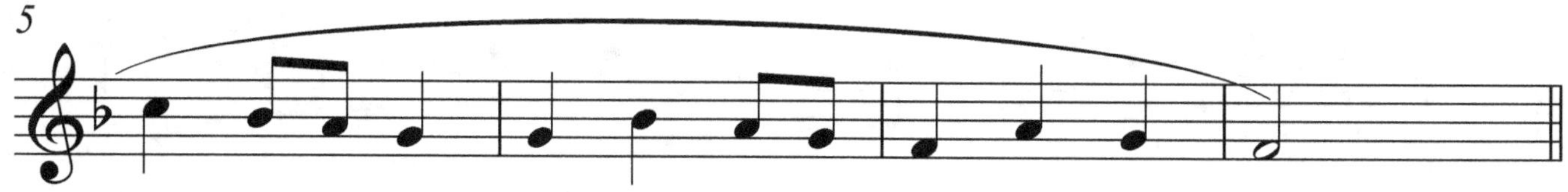
5

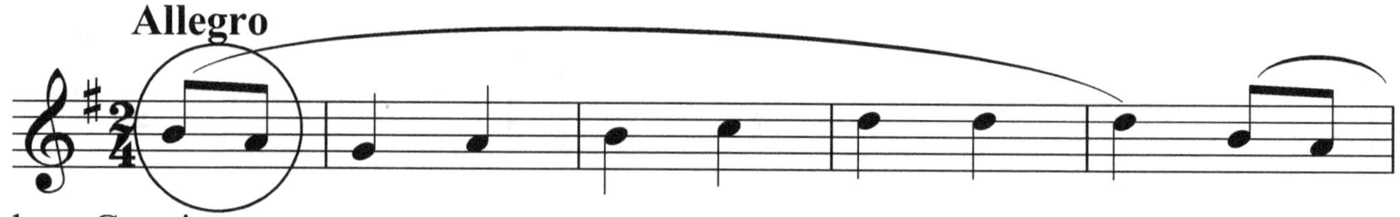
Allegro

key: G major

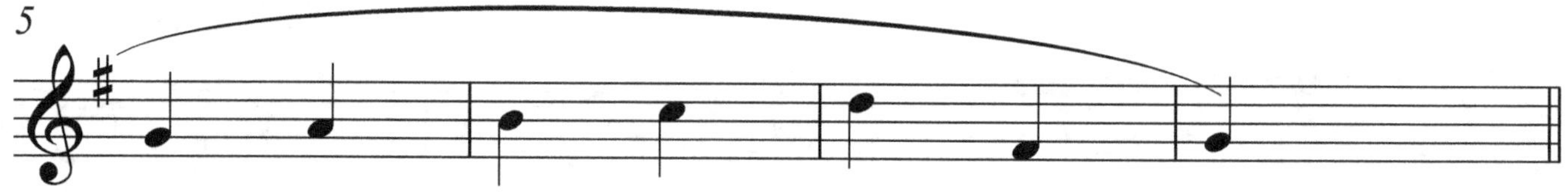
5

Page 156, No. 1

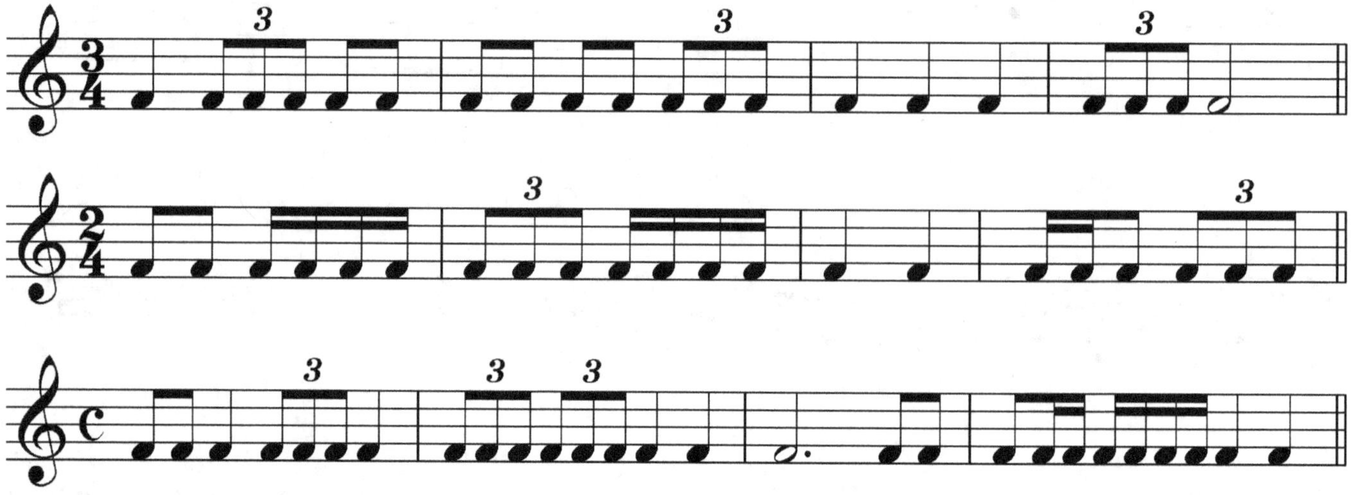

Page 156, No. 2

3/4
2/4
4/4
3/4

Page 158, No. 1

a. Sixteenth note.

b. Eighth note.

c. Half note.

d. Dotted quarter note.

e. Whole note.

f. Quarter note.

Page 158, No. 2

2/4
3/8
2/4
4/4
3/4

Page 159, No. 1

Page 160, No. 2

Lesson 11 - Chords

Page 163, No. 1

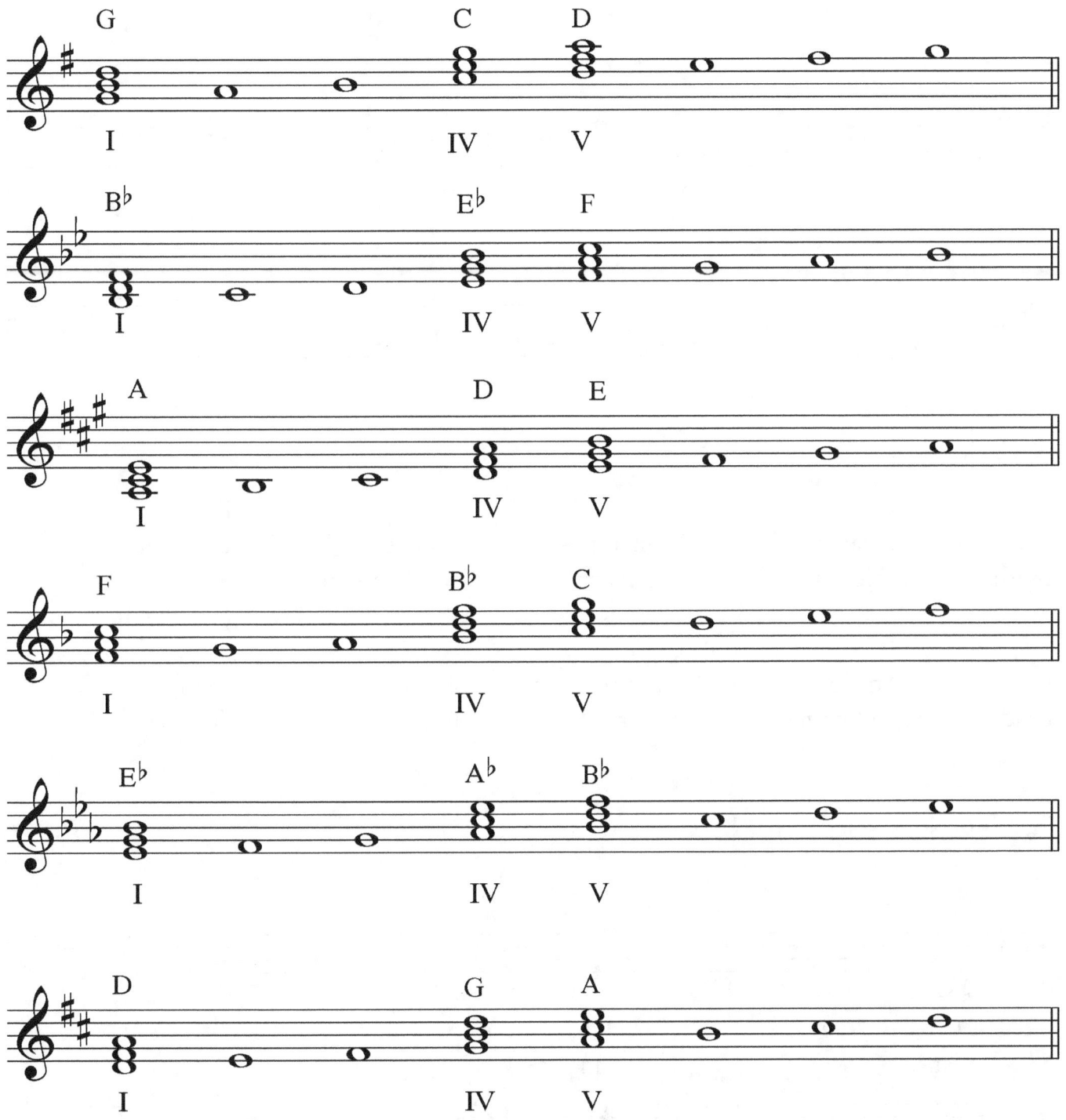

Page 164, No. 2

Page 164, No. 3

	G	F	D	E♭
Key:	G major	B♭ major	A major	E♭ major
Triad:	tonic	dominant	subdominant	tonic

	G	C	A	B♭
Key:	D major	F major	A major	E♭ major
Triad:	subdominant	dominant	tonic	dominant

Page 166, No. 1

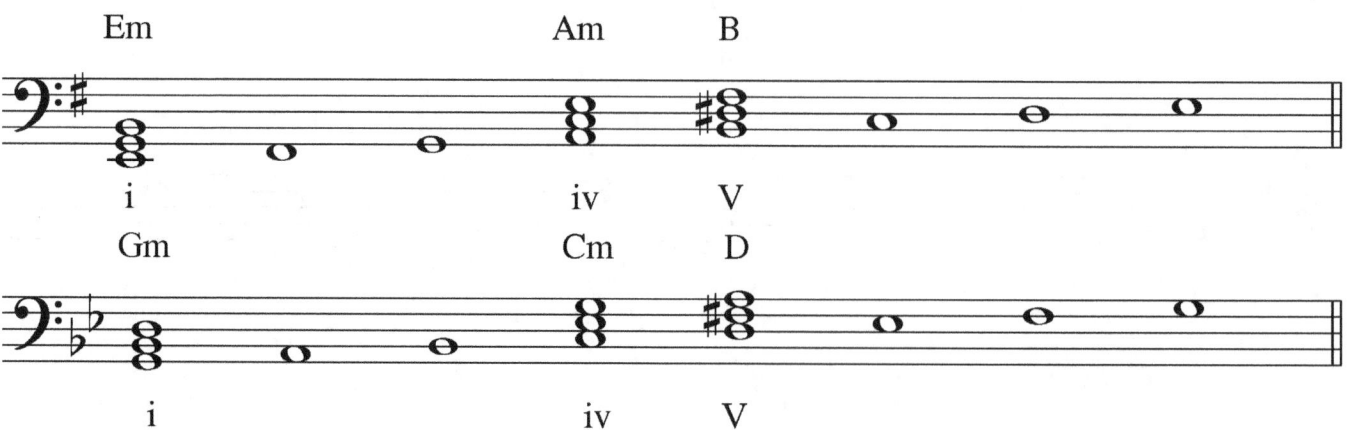

© San Marco Publications 2018

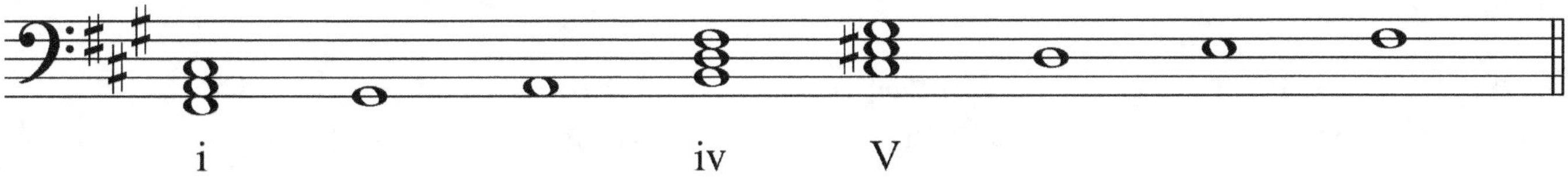
i
iv
V

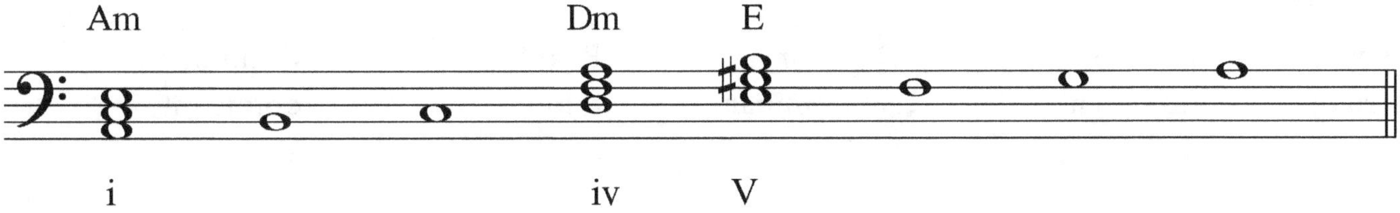
Am
Dm
E
i
iv
V

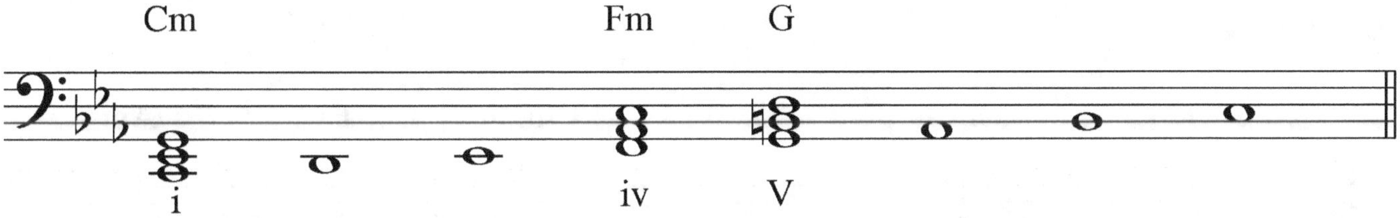
Cm
Fm
G
i
iv
V

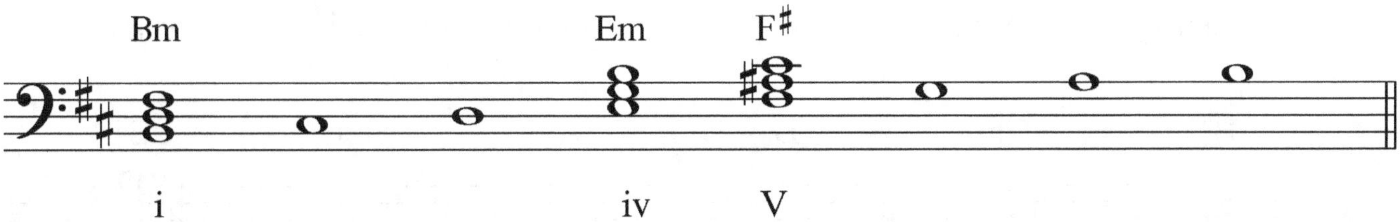
Bm
Em
F♯
i
iv
V

Page 167, No. 2

Dm
D
Fm
Am
i
V
iv
i

F♯
F♯m
Am
B
V
i
iv
V

Cm
C♯
Gm
Em
i
V
iv
i

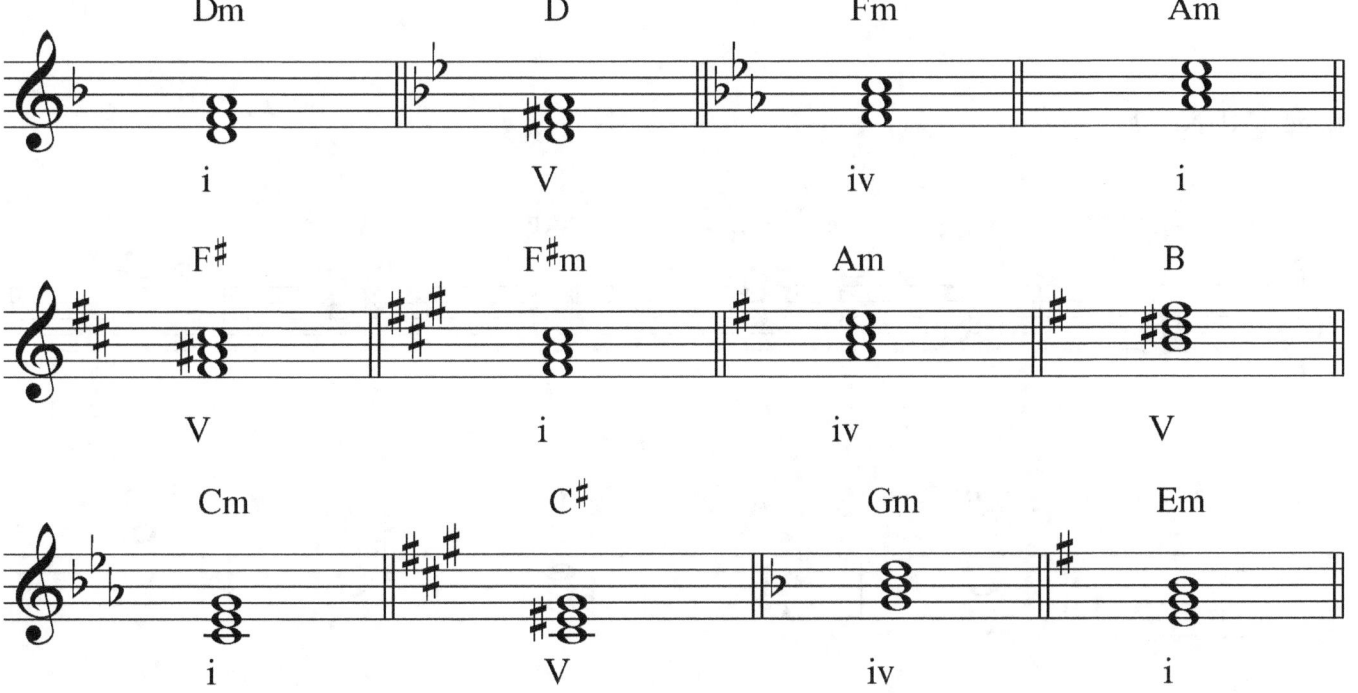

Page 167, No. 3

Key:	E minor	G minor	F# minor	C minor
Triad:	tonic	dominant	subdominant	tonic
	i	V	iv	i

Key:	B minor	D minor	F# minor	C minor
Triad:	dominant	subdominant	tonic	dominant
	V	iv	i	V

Page 170, No. 1

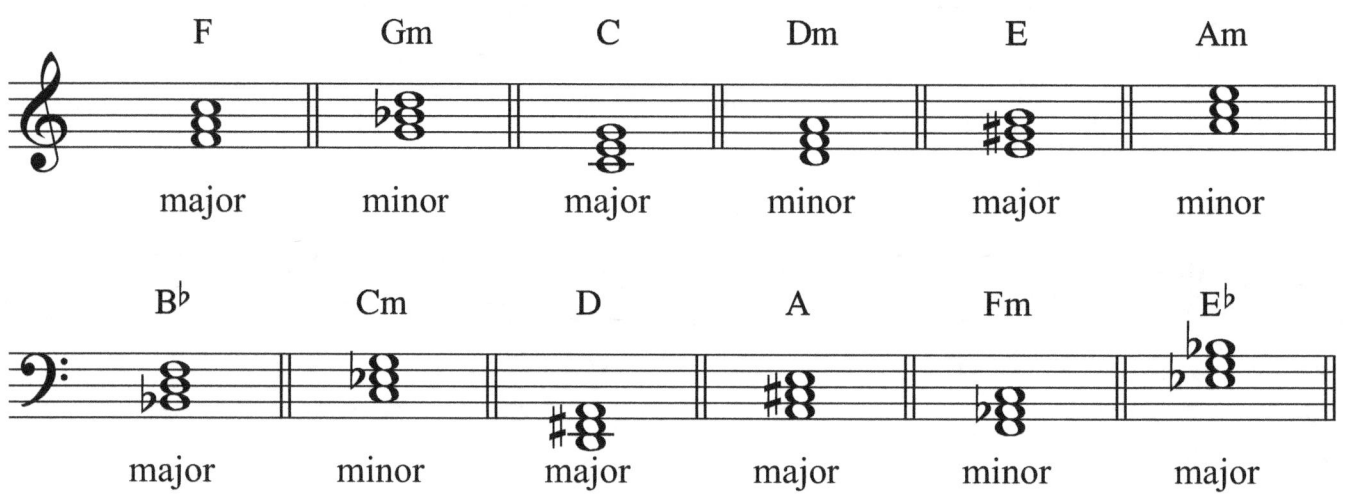

Page 170, No. 2

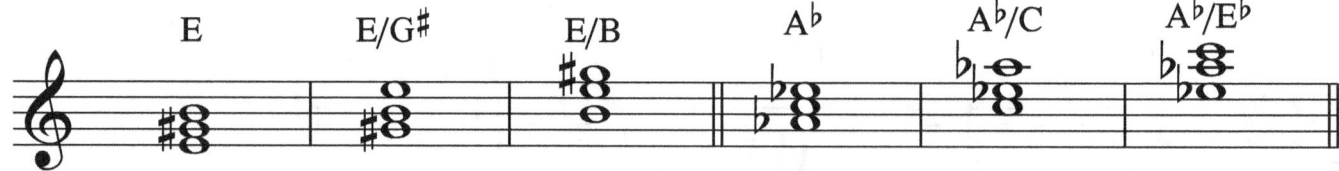

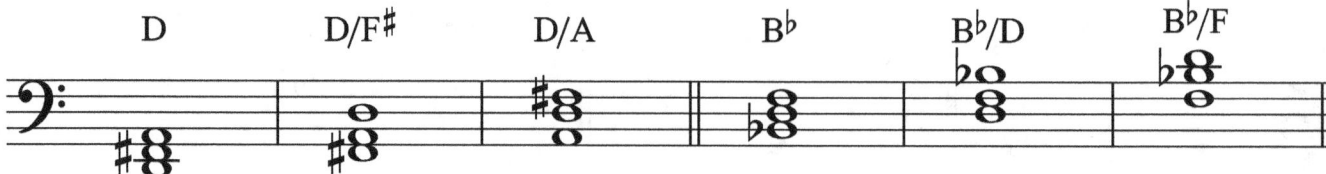

Page 170, No. 3

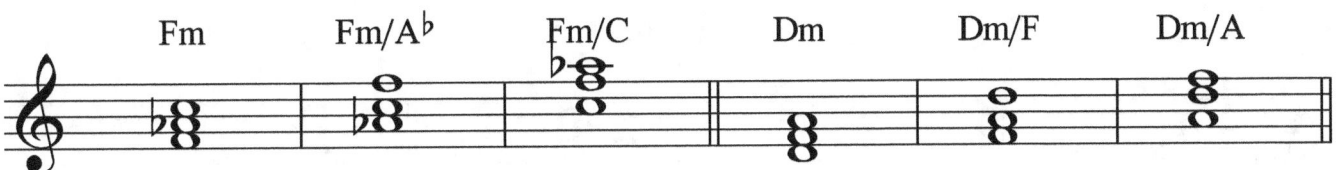

Page 172, No. 1

B♭ C E G D D
F E♭ D E C A

Page 172, No. 2

E	F	G	D	A	A
minor	minor	major	minor	major	minor
2nd inv	1st inc.	root pos.	1st inv.	root pos.	1st inv.

B♭	A♭	B	G	E	F
major	major	minor	minor	minor	major
1st inv.	root pos.	2nd inv.	root pos.	2nd inv.	root pos.

Page 173, No. 3

Page 173, No. 4

Page 174, No. 1

C	B♭	E	G	A	E♭
minor	major	major	major	minor	major
root pos	1st inv	root pos	root pos	1st inv	2nd inv
C#	F	B	G♭	E	F#
major	minor	major	major	minor	minor
root pos	root pos	2nd inv	2nd inv	2nd inv	2nd inv

Page 175, No. 1

Page 175, No. 2

Page 175, No. 3

augmented   major   diminished   augmented   diminished   minor

Page 176, No. 4

F	E♭m	Ddim	Caug	B♭	Am
G♭aug	F#m	C	G#	Adim	D♭aug
Em	Gm	Bdim	D	A♭	Baug

Page 176, No. 5

C	D♭	A	G	F	D
major	augmented	minor	major	diminished	major
1st inv	root pos	1st inv	root pos	2nd inv	root pos

B	G	A♭	F♯	E	C♯
diminished	minor	diminished	major	minor	augmented
2nd inv	2nd inv	root pos	1st inv	root pos	root pos

Page 177, No. 6

F	C♯	A	E♭	D	B
major	minor	diminished	major	augmented	diminished
2nd inv	root pos	1st inv	2nd inv	root pos	1st inv

G	F♯	E♭	B	A	D♭
major	minor	minor	major	minor	major
root pos	2nd inv	2nd inv	root pos	1st inv	2nd inv

C	D	C	D♯	B♭	E
diminished	minor	major	minor	major	minor
root pos	2nd inv	1st inv	root pos	2nd inv	root pos

Page 177, No. 7

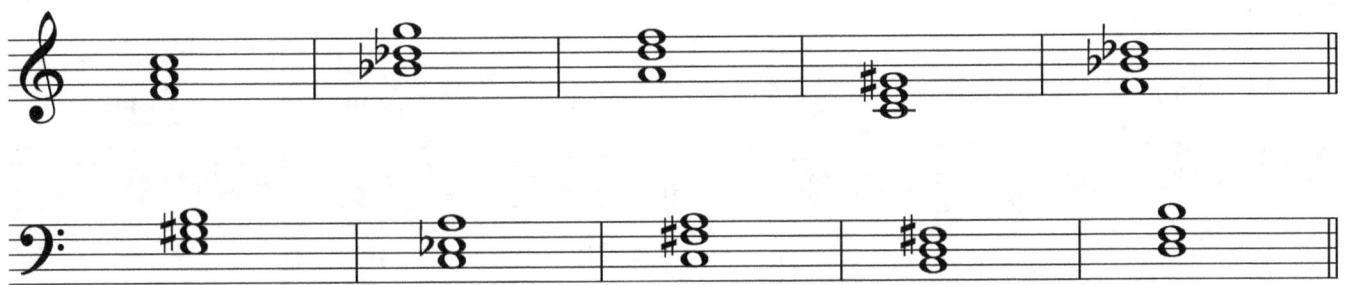

Page 179, No. 1

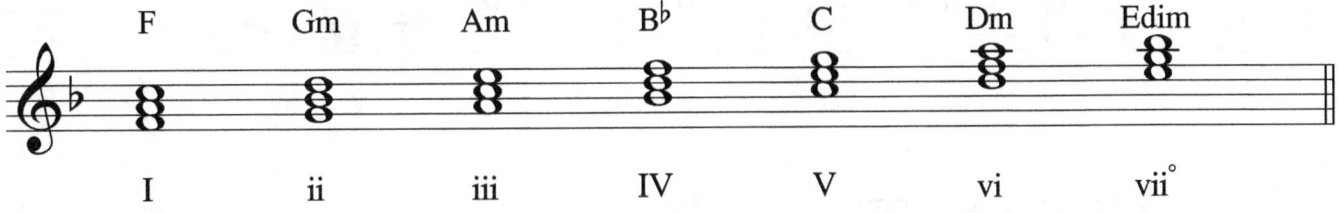

Page 179, No. 2

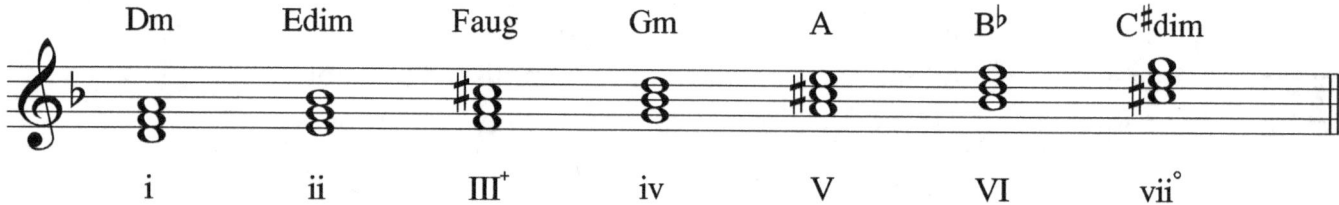

Page 180, No. 3

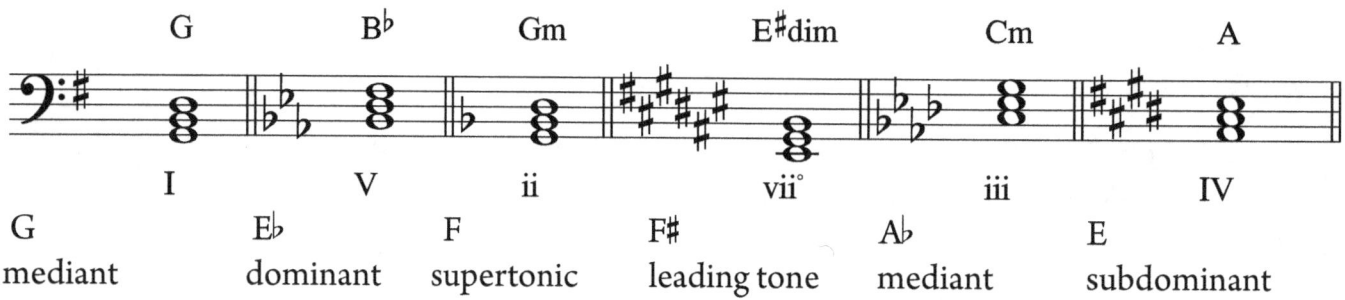

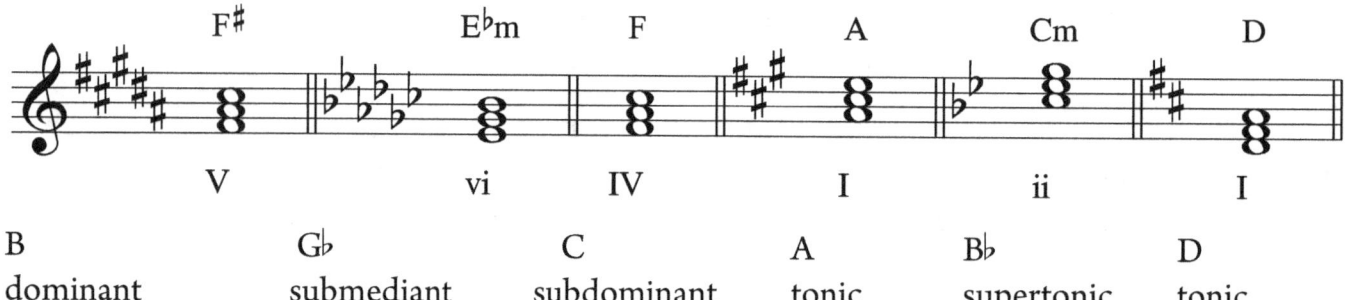

Page 180, No. 4

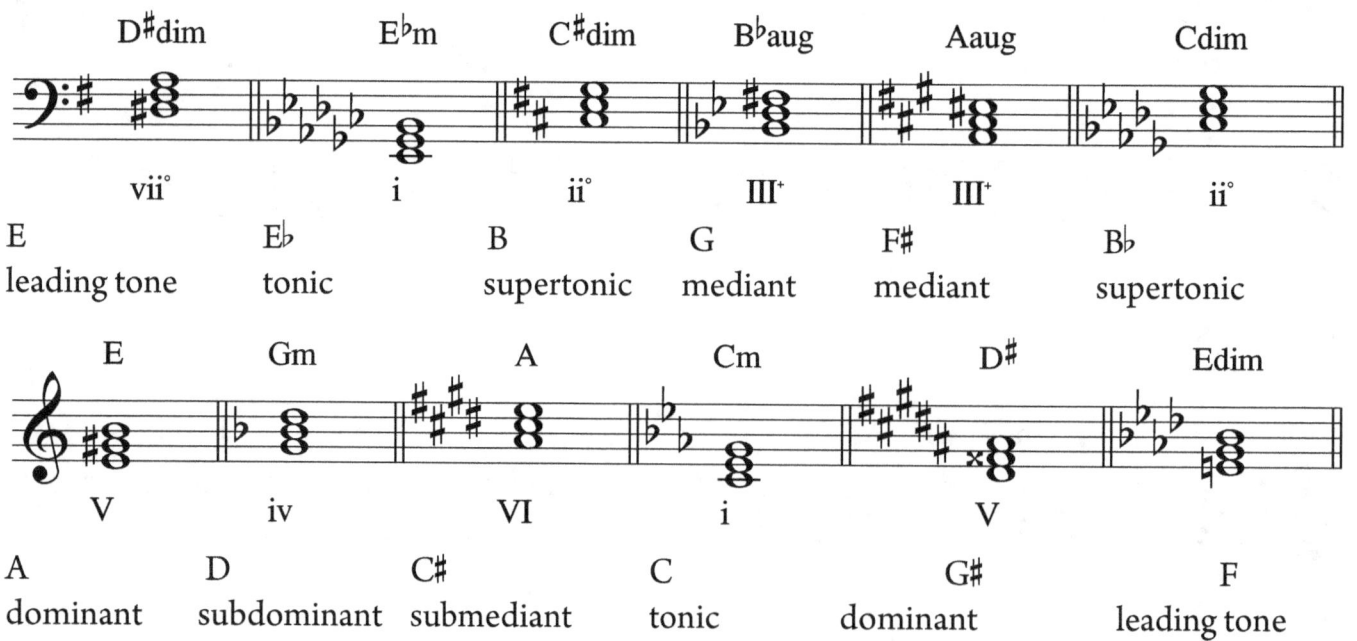

© San Marco Publications 2018

Page 181, No. 5

i.   ii.   iii.   iv.   v.   vi.

Page 181, No. 6

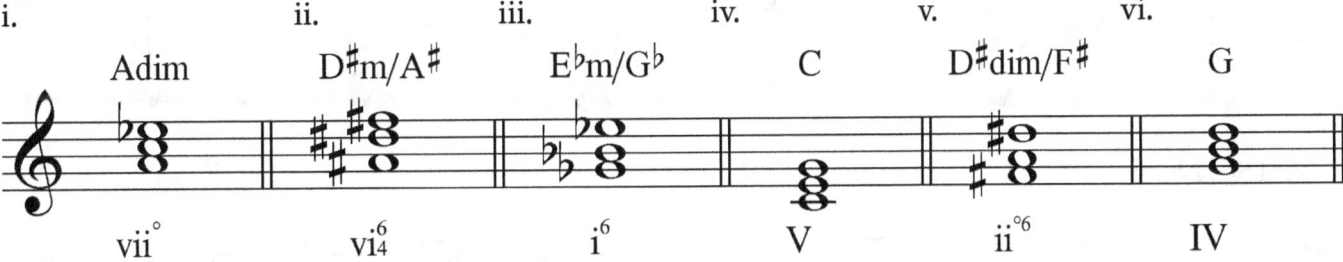

Page 181, No. 7

Page 183, No. 1

Key:	G minor	A major	B minor	F major
Root/quality:	D^7	E^7	$F\#^7$	C^7
Functional:	V^7	V^7	V^7	V^7
Key:	E major	F minor	B major	G major
Root/quality:	B^7	C^7	$F\#^7$	D^7
Functional:	V^7	V^7	V^7	V^7
Key:	E♭ major	D major	A minor	B♭ minor
Root/quality:	$B♭^7$	A^7	E^7	F^7
Functional:	V^7	V^7	V^7	V^7

Page 183, No. 2

| F major | D major | E♭ major | G major | B major | A major |
| F minor | D minor | E♭ minor | G minor | B minor | A minor |

Page 184, No. 1

D major   G major   C major   F major   B♭ major   E♭ major

Page 184, No. 2

Page 184, No. 3

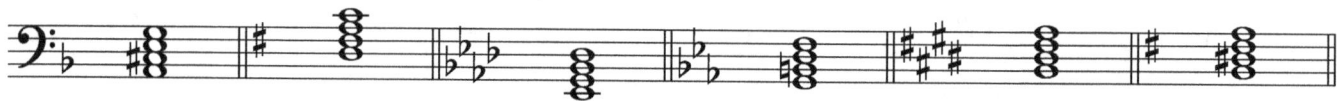

Page 184, No. 4

F major   C major   B♭ major   E♭ major   A major   E major

Page 186, No. 1

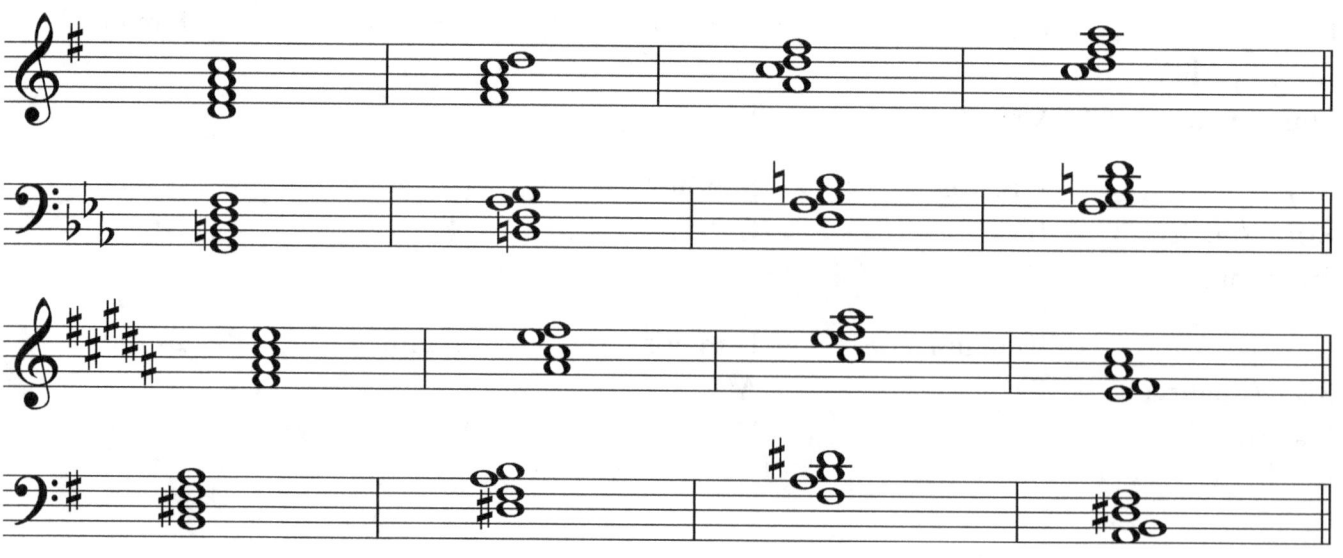

Page 186-187, No. 2

A♭	G	F	D	E	D♭
D♭ major	C major	B♭ major	G major	A major	G♭ major
D♭ minor	C minor	B♭ minor	G minor	A minor	G♭ minor
root pos	2nd inv	1st inv	3rd inv	1st inv	2nd inv

F♯	A♭	C	A	G♭	B♭
B major	D♭ major	F major	D major	C♭ major	E♭ major
B minor	D♭ minor	F minor	D minor	C♭ minor	E♭ minor
root pos	1st inv	3rd inv	1st inv	root pos	1st inv

Page 187, No. 3 (other answers are possible)

F major   G major   C major   E♭ major   E major   A major

F♯ major   B♭ major   E♭ major   A♭ major   G♭ major   B major

Page 187-188, No. 4

D	C	G	B	F♯	E♭
G major	F major	C minor	E major	B minor	A♭ major
root pos	1st inv	1st inv	2nd inv	root pos	3rd inv

F♯	B	D	F	A	A
B major	E minor	G minor	B♭ minor	D major	D minor
root pos	2nd inv	2nd inv	root pos	2nd inv	1st inv

Page 189, No. 1

D♯dim⁷	F♯dim⁷	E♯dim⁷	C♯dim	Bdim⁷	F𝑥dim⁷
E minor	G minor	F♯ minor	D minor	C minor	G♯ minor
vii°⁷	vii°⁷	vii°⁷	vii°⁷	vii°⁷	vii°⁷

© San Marco Publications 2018

Page 189, No. 2

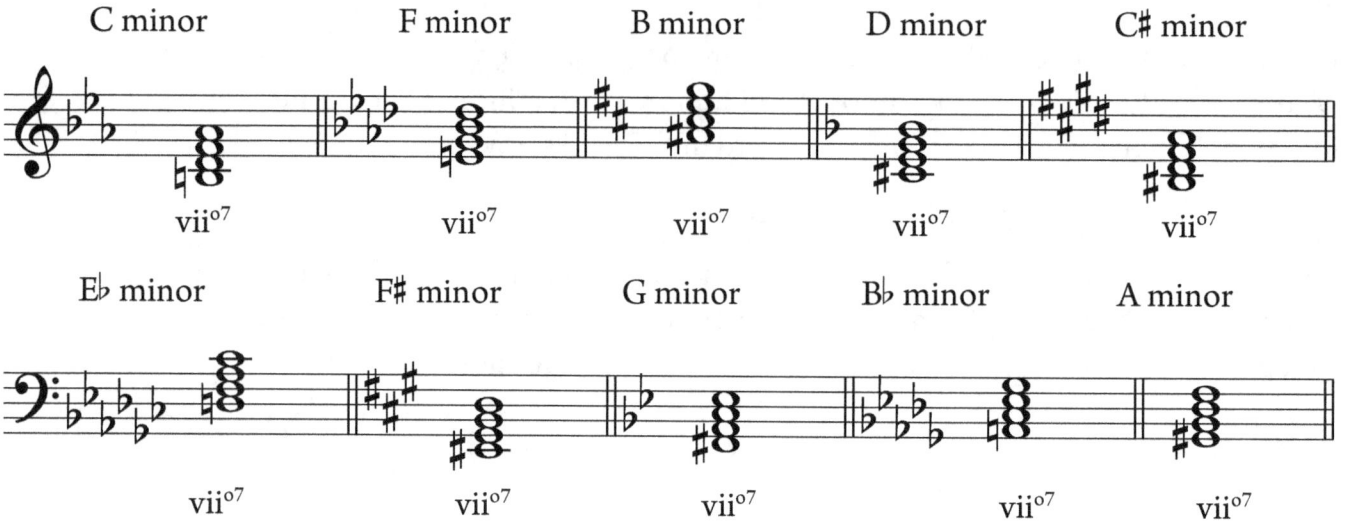

Page 189, No. 3

Page 190, No. 4

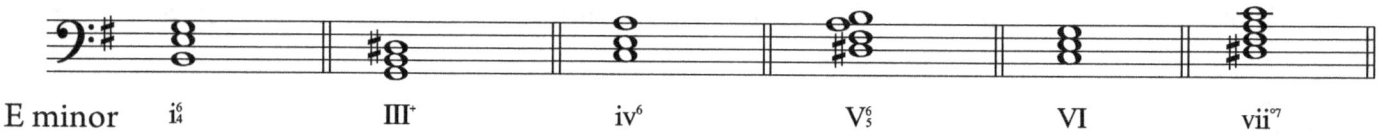

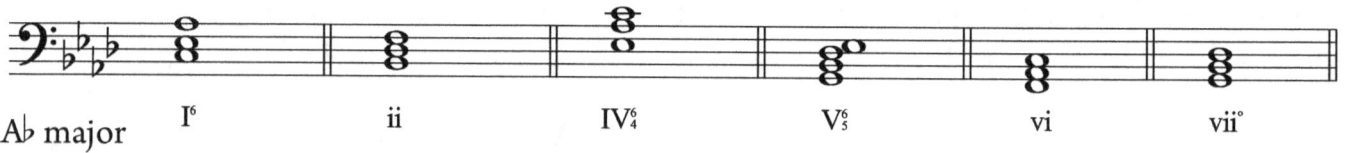

Page 192, No. 1

e. d. a. h. f. b. c. g.

Page 195-196, No. 1

A major:	A major root pos $\hat{1}$	D major root pos $\hat{4}$	A major root pos $\hat{1}$

C major:	C major root pos $\hat{1}$	G major 1st inv $\hat{5}$	A minor root pos $\hat{6}$	D minor 1st inv $\hat{2}$

A minor:	A minor root pos $\hat{1}$	E major root pos $\hat{5}$

G major:	G major root pos $\hat{1}$	D major 1st inv $\hat{5}$

E minor:	E minor root pos $\hat{1}$	B major root pos $\hat{5}$

Lesson 12 - Cadences

Page 199-200, No. 1

	E A V I			F B♭ V I
A major:	perfect authentic		B♭ major:	imperfect authentic

	G C V I			G Cm V i
C major:	perfect authentic		C minor:	imperfect authentic

B E		A Dm	
V I		V i	
E major: perfect authentic		D minor: perfect authentic	

F B♭m		B Em	
V i		V i	
B♭ minor: imperfect authentic		E minor: perfect authentic	

Page 202, No. 1

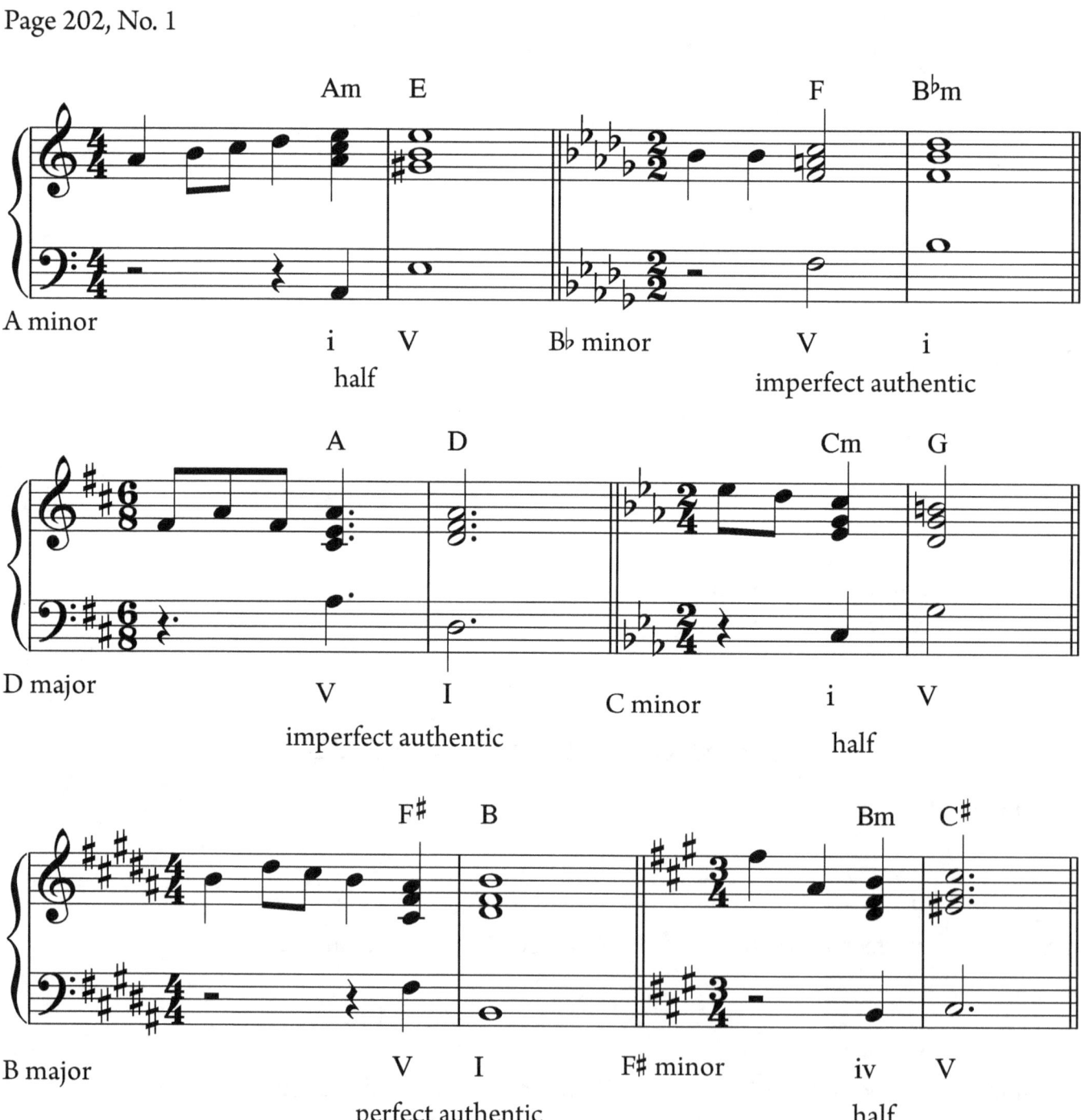

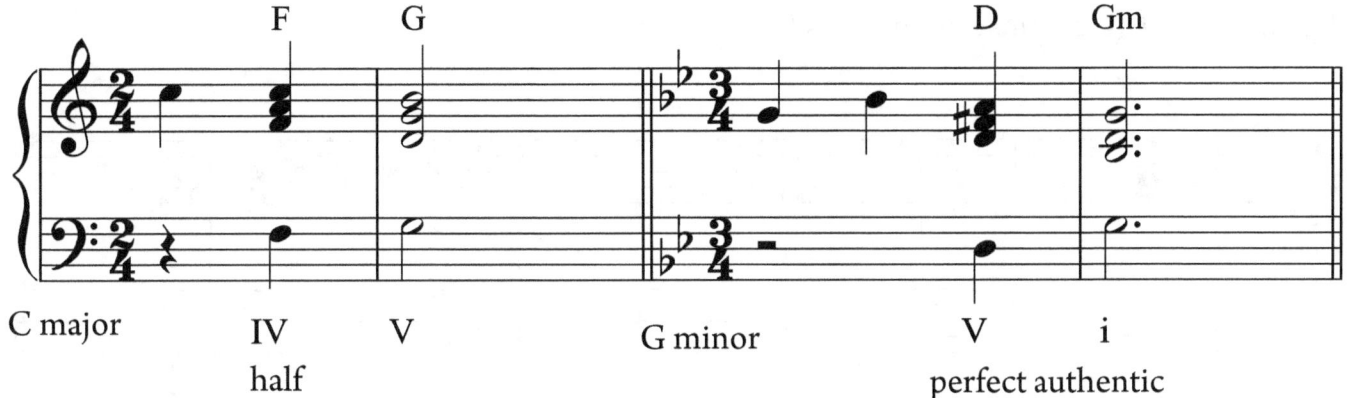

Page 206, No. 1 (other answers are possible)

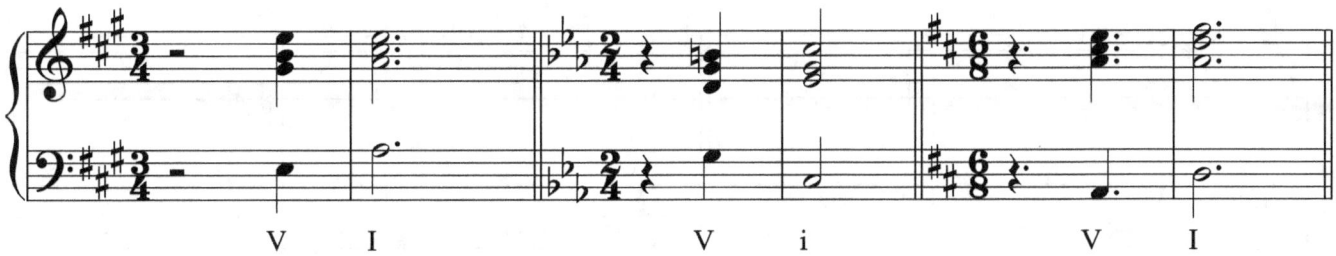

Page 206, No. 2 (other answers are possible)

Page 206, No. 3 (other answers are possible)

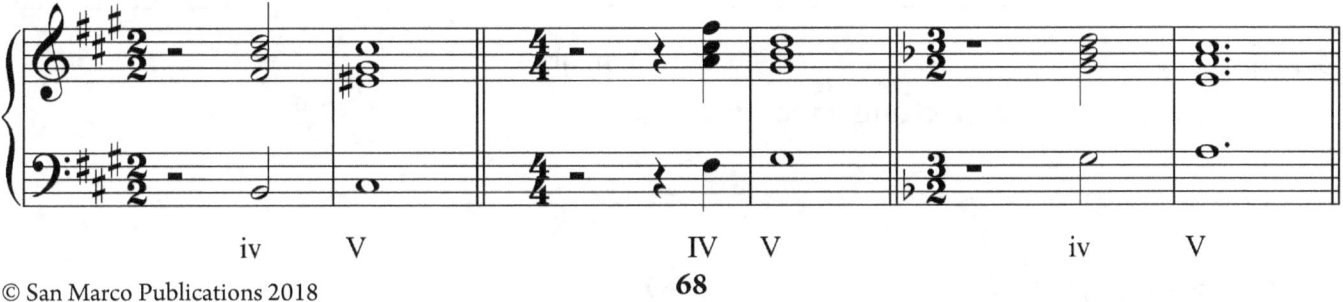

© San Marco Publications 2018

Page 209, No. 1 (other answers are possible)

Page 210 (other answers are possible)

Page 211, No. 2 (other answers are possible)

Page 212-213, No. 1

	Gm Dm			F B♭
	iv i			V I
D minor:	plagal		B♭ major:	perfect authentic

	A E			Fm Cm
	IV I			iv i
E major:	plagal		C minor:	plagal

	Am E			E♭m B♭m
	i V			iv i
A minor:	half		B♭ minor:	plagal

	A D			Cm G
	V I			i V
D major:	imperfect authentic		C minor:	half

	E B			Bm C#
	IV I			iv V
B major:	plagal		F# minor:	half

	F G			D Gm
	IV V			V i
C major:	half		G minor:	perfect authentic

Page 215, No. 1 (other answers are possible)

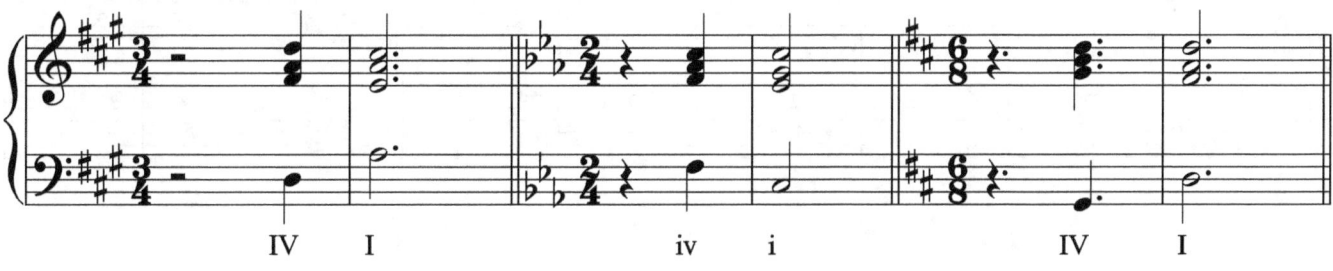

Page 219, No. 1 (other answers are possible)

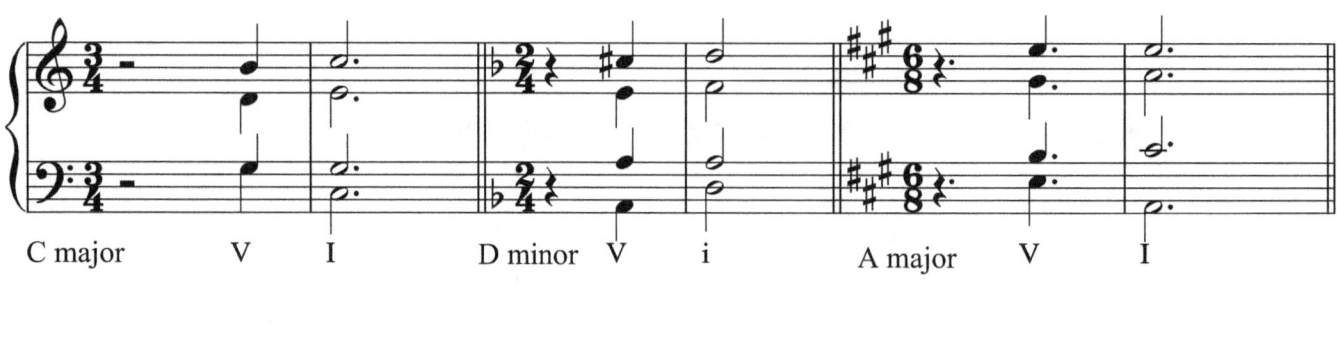

Page 219, No. 2 (other answers are possible)

Page 221, No. 1 (other answers are possible)

© San Marco Publications 2018

Page 222, No. 2

Page 223, No. 3

D minor

i V
half

V i
perfect authentic

Lesson 13 - Meter 2

Page 224, No. 1

3/4	3/4
2/4	2/4
4/4	4/4
3/4	4/4
2/4	3/4

Page 226, No. 1

2/4   2/2   2/4   2/8   2/2   2/8   2/4

Page 228, No. 1

George Frideric Handel
Water Music, X

Joseph Haydn
Symphony No. 92

© San Marco Publications 2018

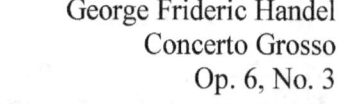

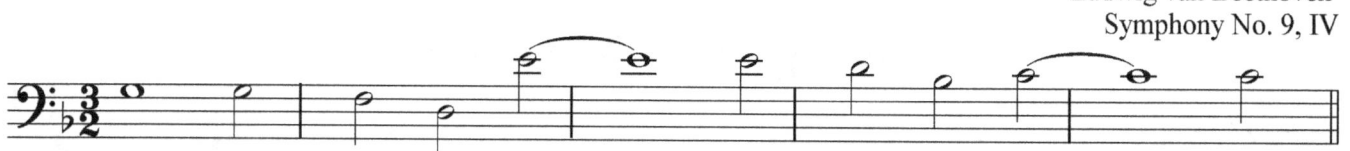

Page 230, No. 1

4/2   4/4   4/2   4/4

Page 231, No. 2

Page 231, No. 3

4/4   4/2   3/2

© San Marco Publications 2018

Page 232, No. 1

Page 232, No. 2

Page 233, No. 1

Page 234, No. 1

2/2   3/4   4/2   4/4

Page 235, No. 2

Page 235, No. 3

© San Marco Publications 2018

Page 238, No. 1

Page 239, No. 2

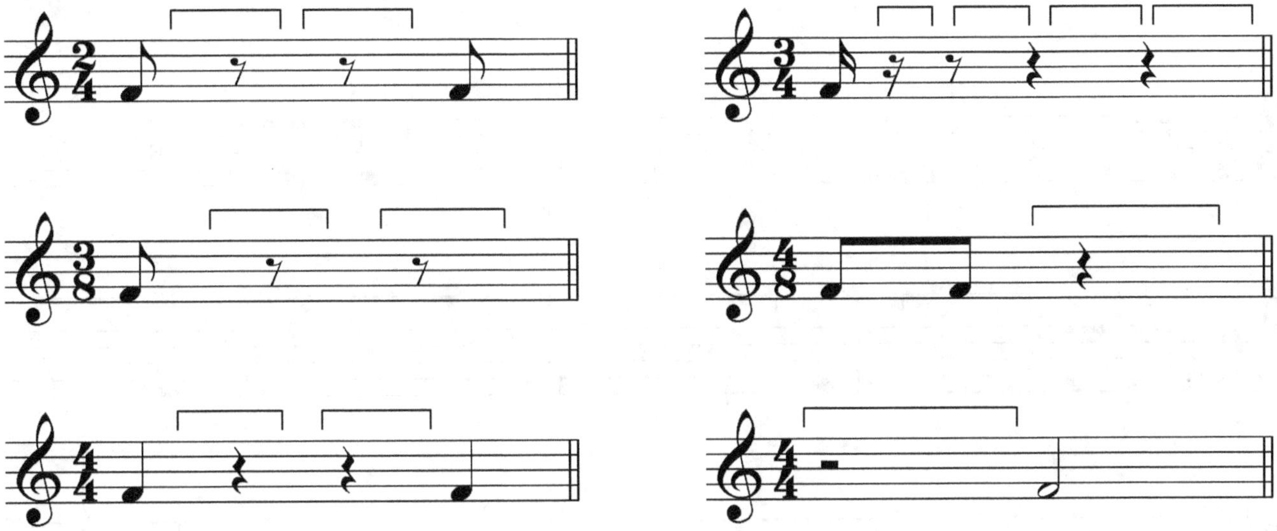

Page 239, No. 2

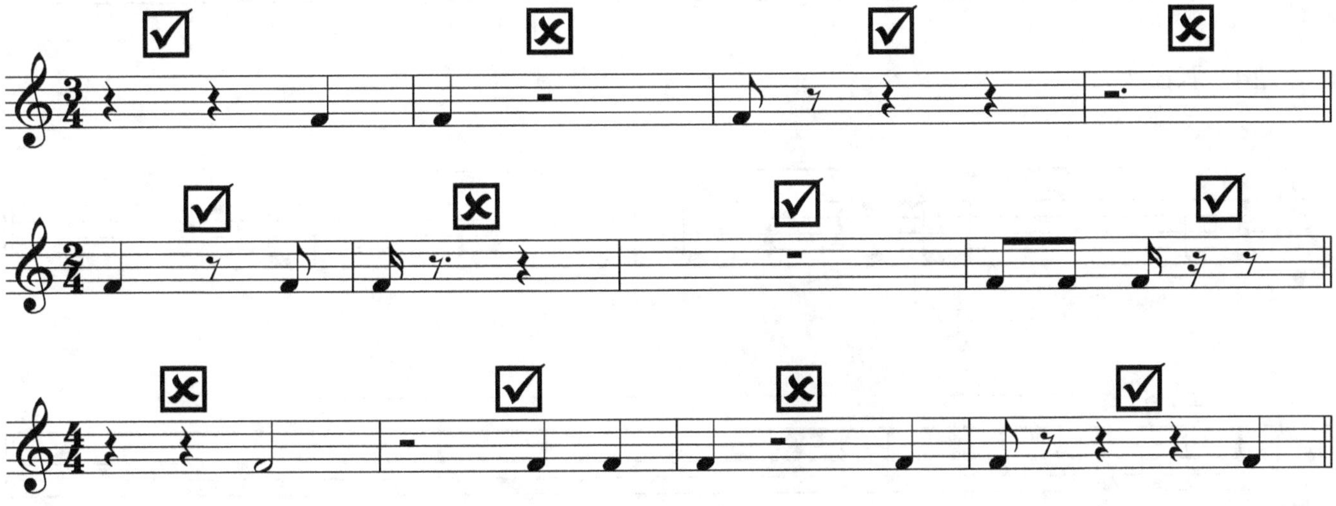

Page 240, No. 3

Page 241, No. 4

Page 243, No. 1

Page 244, No. 2

Edvard Grieg
Norwegian Melody

Robert Schumann
Symphony No. 3

Gustav Mahler
Resurrection Symphony No. 1

Page 246, No. 1

Samual Arnold
Gigue

Ludvig Schytte
Etude

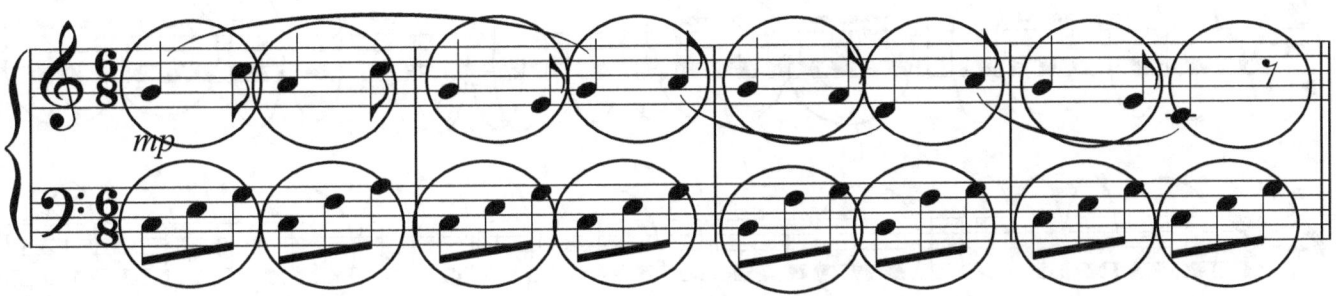

Page 247, No. 2

Page 248, No. 2

Page 249, No. 3

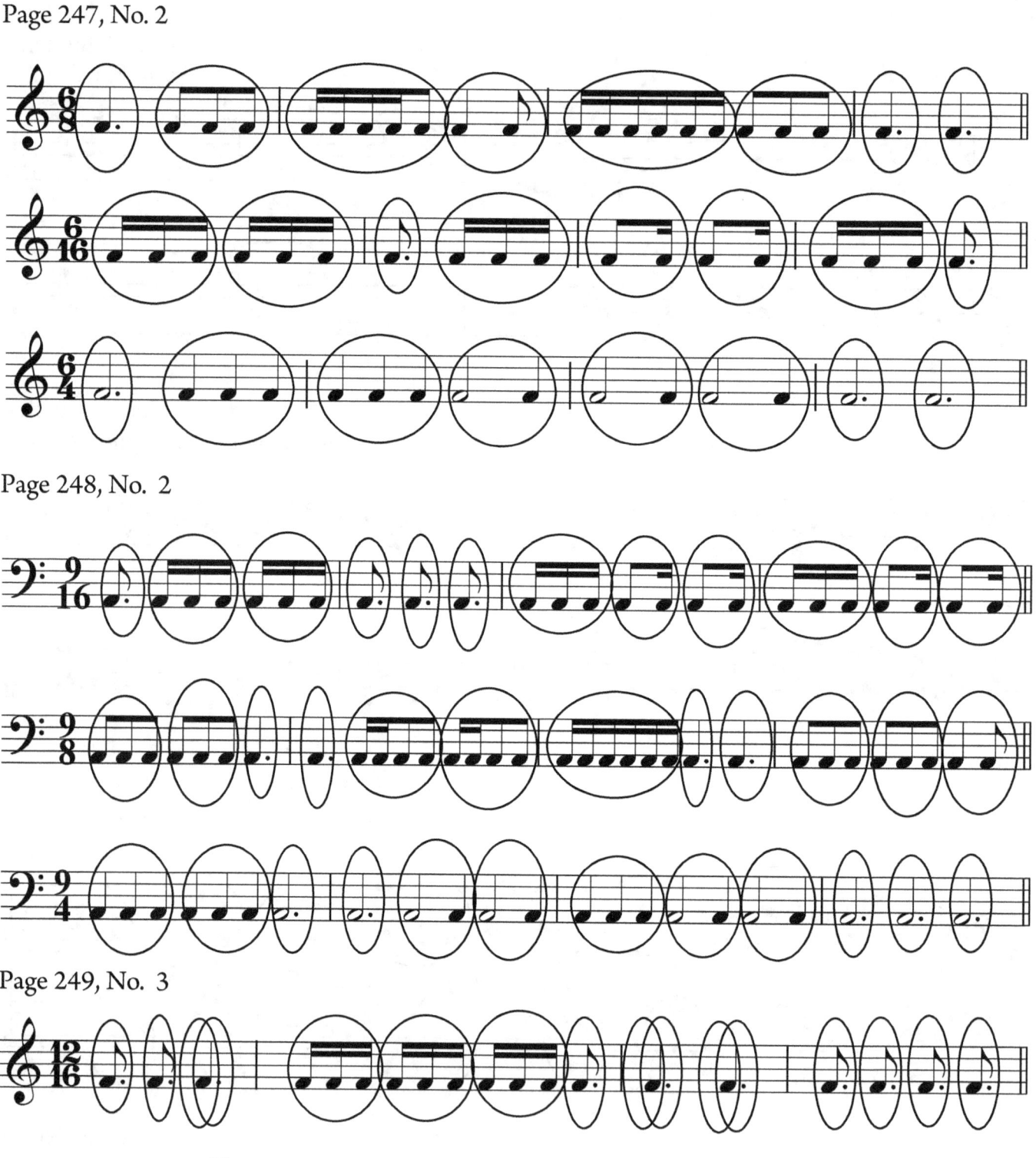

Page 250, No. 4

Page 252-253, No. 5

Page 253-254, No. 6

12/8
6/8
3/2
9/8
4/2
4/4
6/8
2/4
9/8
12/8

Page 256, No. 1

2, 3, 3, 3, 6, 7, 7, 7

Page 256, No. 2 and 3

Page 258, No. 1

Page 259-260, No. 1

Giacomo Puccini
Madam Butterfly (One Fine Day)

Lili Boulanger
Nocturne

Page 263, No. 1

Page 264, No. 2

Page 264, No. 3

Page 267, No. 1 (other answers are possible)

Lesson 14 - Transposition

Page 269, No. 1

Felix Mendelssohn
Song Without Words "Faith"

Giuseppe Verdi
March from Aida

Page 270, No. 2

William Byrd
Pavan

J. S. Bach
Toccata and Fugue in G minor

Page 271, No. 3

Dimitri Shostakovich
Symphony No.7, Op. 60

J.S. Bach
Fugue 24 From WTC Book 2

Page 271, No. 4

Frederic Chopin
Sonata in G minor

Claude Debussy
Petite Suite

© San Marco Publications 2018

Page 277, No. 1

F major

Page 279, No. 1

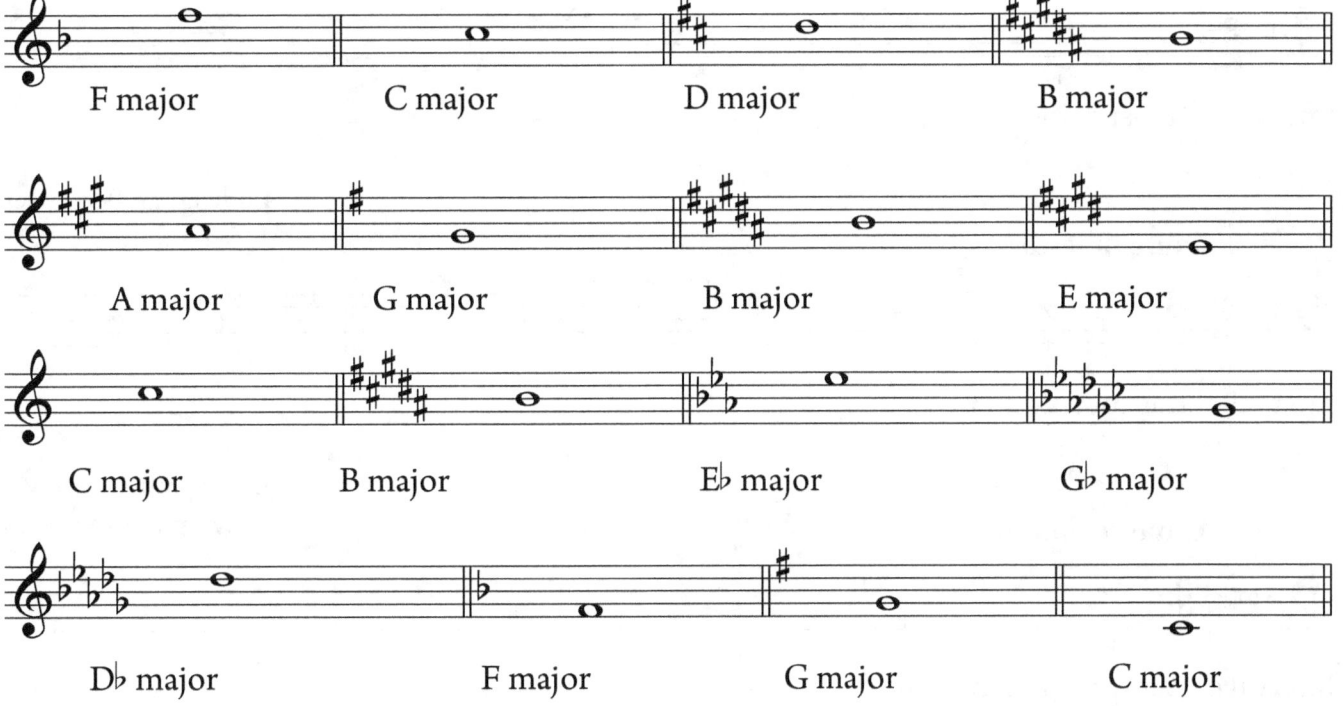

Ludwig van Beethoven
Symphony No. 9, IV

Andante maestoso

Interval of transposition: maj 2

Page 283, No. 1

C major

Wolfgang Amadeus Mozart
Clarinet Concerto, K. 622

Allegro

B♭ major

Page 284, No. 2

E♭ major

Johann Nepomuk Hummel
Trumpet Concerto, III

Allegro

F major

Page 284, No. 3

A minor

Wolfgang Amadeus Mozart
Symphony No. 40, Minuet

Allegretto

G minor

Page 285, No. 1

B♭ major

Wolfgang Amadeus Mozart
Concerto for Horn, K.447, III

Allegro

E♭ major

© San Marco Publications 2018

Page 286, No. 2

G minor

Wolfgang Amadeus Mozart
Allegro, K.312

A minor

Wolfgang Amadeus Mozart
Allegro, K.312

D minor

C# minor

Antono Vivaldi
The Four Seasons, Spring

G# minor

Antono Vivaldi
The Four Seasons, Spring

D# minor

Lesson 15 - Score Types

Page 295, No. 1

Johann Sebastian Bach
Chorale no. 67: Freu'dich sehr, o meine Seele

Page 296, No. 2

Johann Sebastian Bach
Das walt' mein gott

Page 297, No. 3

Ludwig van Beethoven
String Quartet Op 18, No. 1

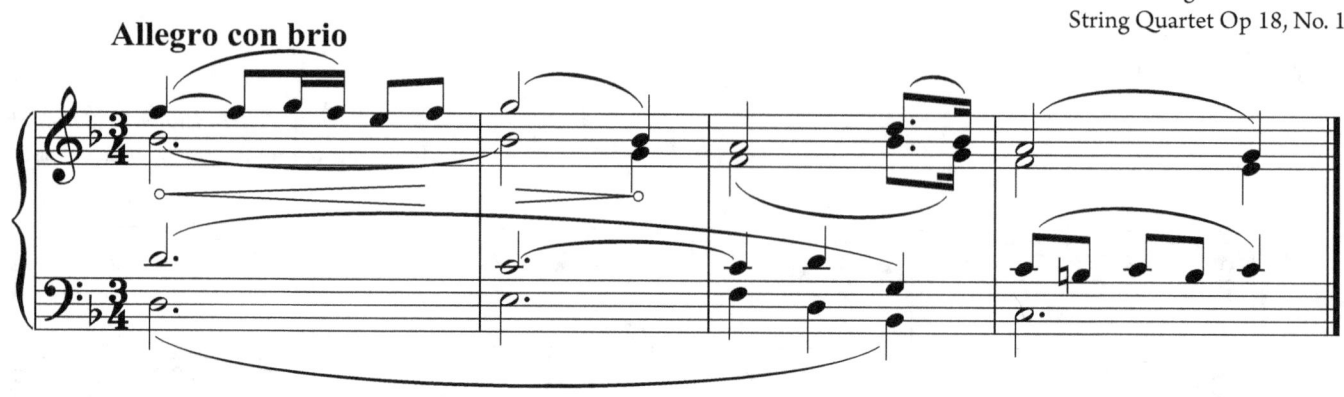

Page 298, No. 4

Franz Joseph Haydn
String Quartet Op 76, No. 3

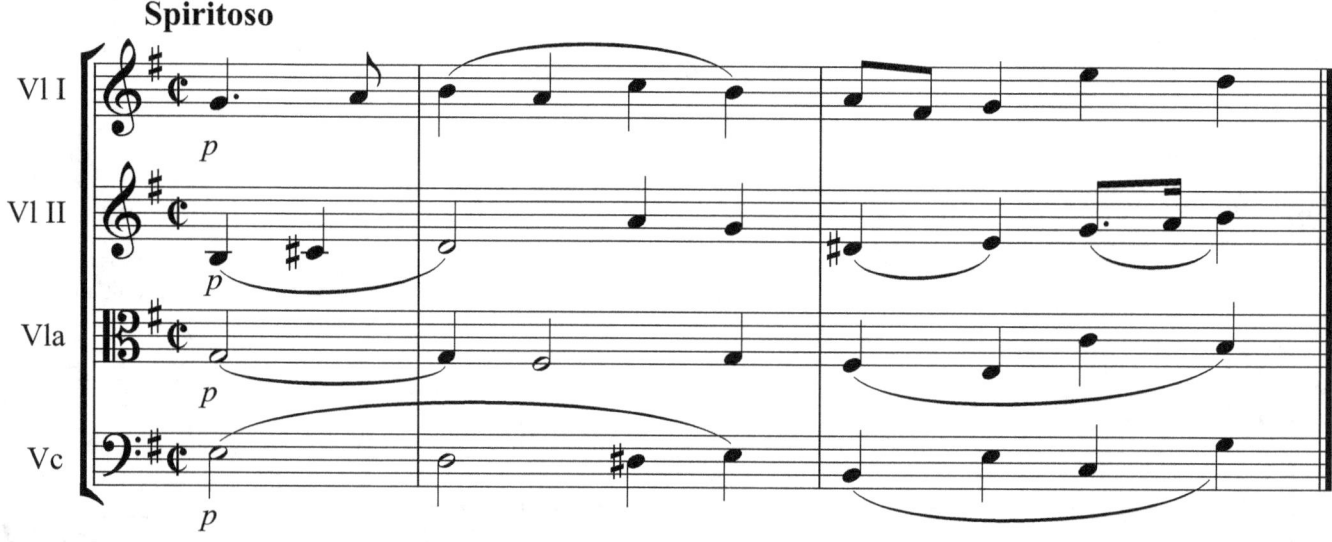

Page 299, No. 5

Johann Sebastian Bach
O Haupt Voll und Wunden

© San Marco Publications 2018

Lesson 16 - Melody

Page 301, No. 1

key: F major

key: C major

Page 303, No.1

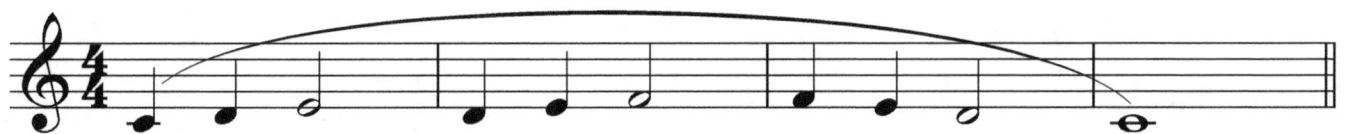

Page 303, No. 2

Page 303, No.3

Page 305, No. 1

F major	$\hat{2}$	unstable
C major	$\hat{1}$	stable
G major	$\hat{3}$	stable
E♭ major	$\hat{1}$	stable
E major	$\hat{2}$	unstable

© San Marco Publications 2018

Page 308, No. 1

Page 308, No. 2

Page 308, No. 3

Page 310, No. 1

F major

C major

G major

Page 310, No. 2

key: C major

key: G major

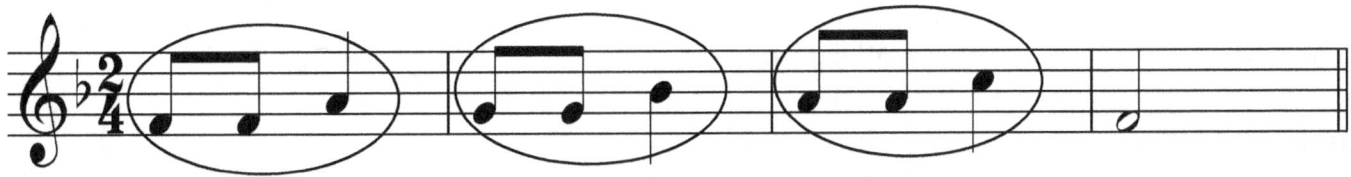

key: F major

Page 312, No. 1

key: G major

The first phrase ends on: ☐ a stable scale degree ☑ an unstable scale degree

The second phrase ends on: ☑ a stable scale degree ☐ an unstable scale degree

This is a: ☑ parallel period ☐ contrasting period

Page 313, No. 2

key: F major

The first phrase ends on: ☐ a stable scale degree   ☑ an unstable scale degree

The second phrase ends on: ☑ a stable scale degree   ☐ an unstable scale degree

This is a: ☐ parallel period   ☑ contrasting period

Page 314, No. 1

Page 317, No. 1

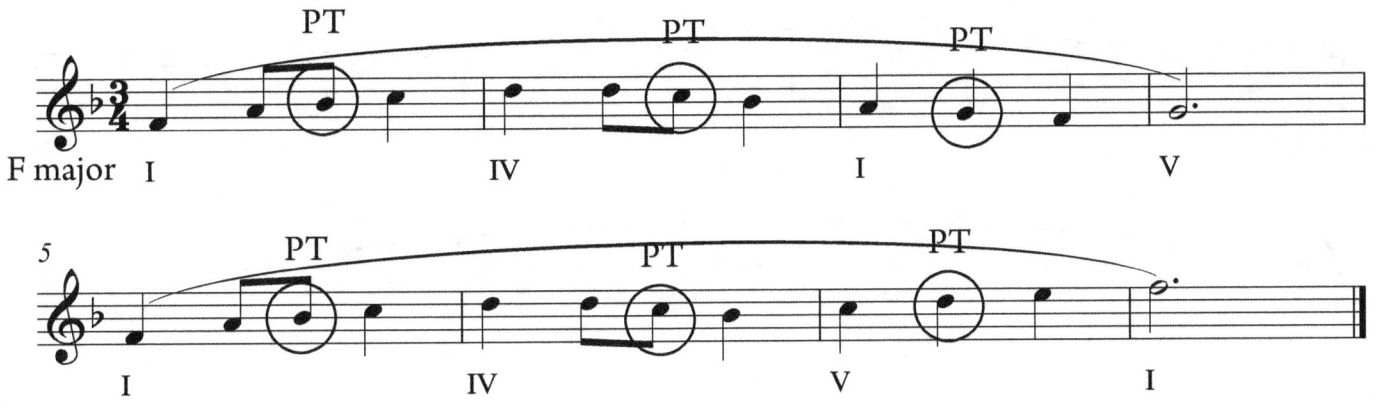

Page 321, No. 1

Page 324, No. 1

Page 325, No. 2 (other answers are possible)

Page 328-329, No. 1 (other answers are possible)

a

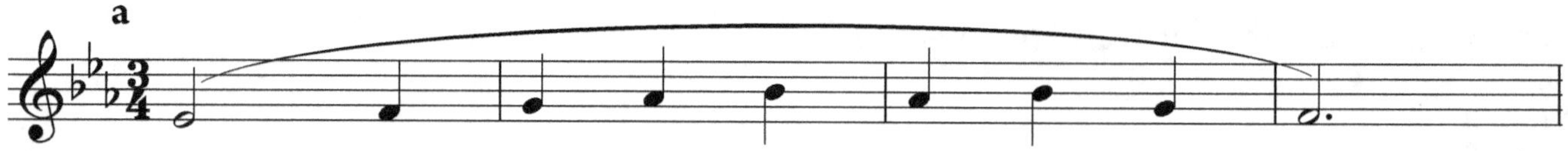

E♭ major

half

b

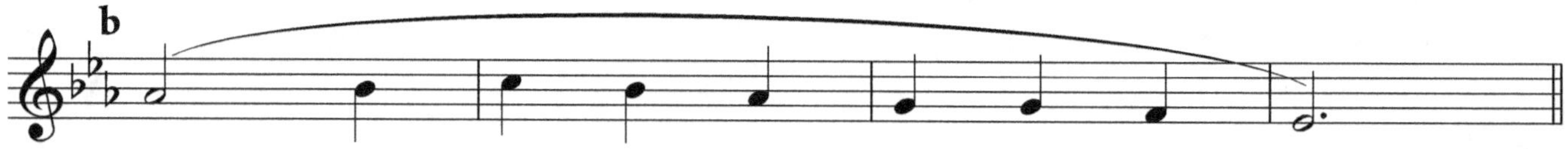

perfect authentic

a

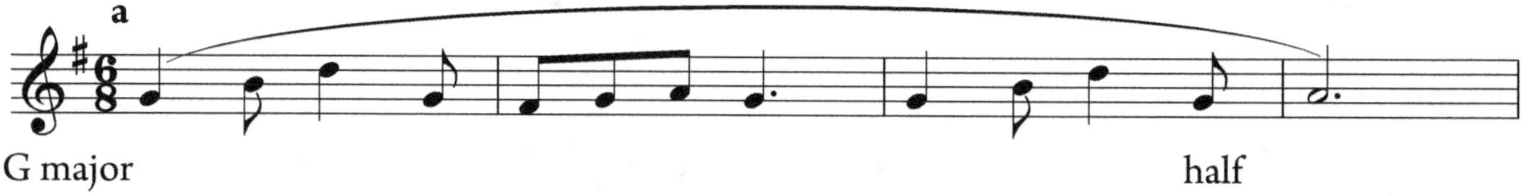

G major

half

b

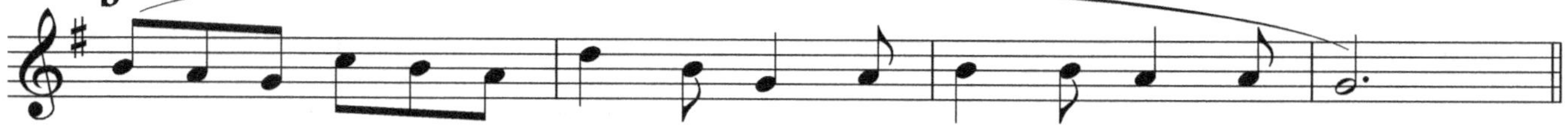

perfect authentic

a

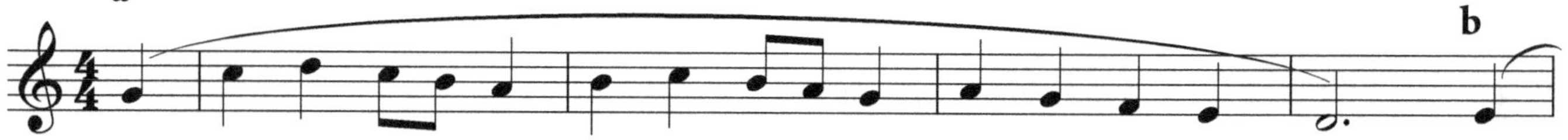

half

C major

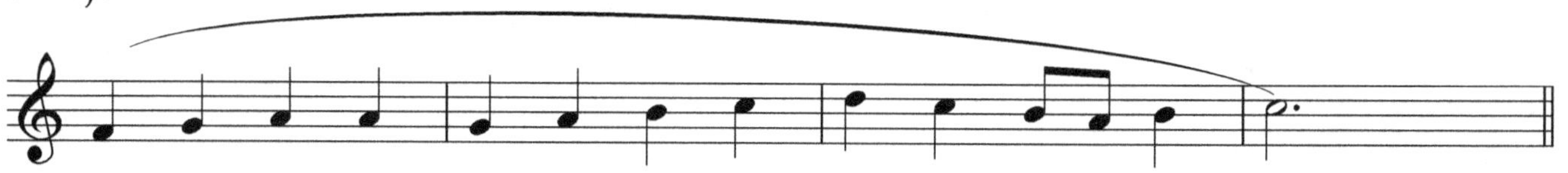

perfect authentic

Page 333, No. 1

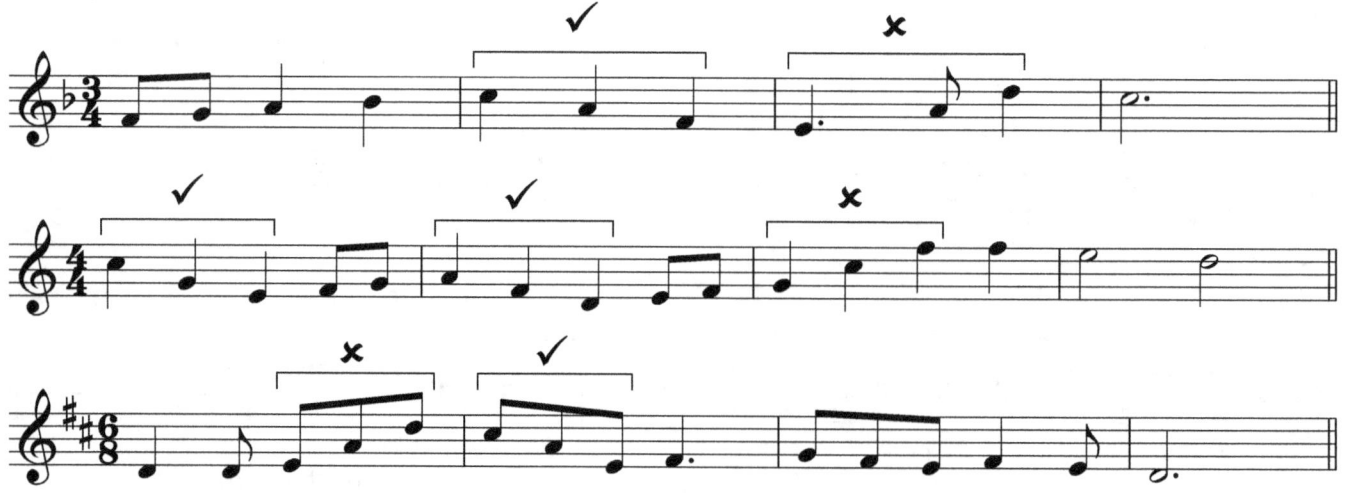

Page 338, No. 2 (other answers are possible)

Page 339, No. 3 (other answers are possible)

Lesson 17 - Music Analysis

Page 340, No. 1

a. Add the correct time signature directly on the music.

b. Name the key of this piece. **F major**

c. Circle a complete F major scale in this piece.

d. Draw a phrase mark over the phrase.

e. On which scale degree does this phrase end? **1̂**

f. Is this a stable degree? **yes**

g. Define *Allegro*. **fast**

h. Explain the sign at letter A. **fortissimo, very loud**

i. Explain the sign at letter B. **fermata, pause**

j. Label all the leading tones **LT.**

Page 342-343, No. 1

Irish Air

American Folk Tune

Carol based on Chant
"O Come, O Come Emmanuel"

Allegro

Alexander Reinagle
(1756 - 1809)

a. Add the correct time signature directly on the music.

b. Name the key of this piece. **C major**

c. Name the composer of this piece. **Alexander Reinagle**

d. Draw a phrase mark over each phrase.

e. Label the phrases according to the form (a, a¹, b)

f. These two phrases for a: ☑ contrasting period   ☐ parallel period

g. Does the second phrase end on a stable or unstable degree? **stable**

h. Define *Allegro*. **fast**

i. How are measure 1 and 2 similar to 5 and 6? **The rhythm is the same.**

i. Locate and circle a half step in this piece.

Page 345

Carefree

Daniel Gottlob Turk
((1756 - 1813))

a. Add the correct time signature directly on the music.

b. Name the key of this piece. **G major**

c. Name the composer of this piece. **Daniel Gottlob Turk**

d. Draw a phrase mark over each phrase.

e. Label the phrases according to the form (a, a¹, b)

f. These two phrases for a: ☐ contrasting period   ☑ parallel period

g. Does the second phrase end on a stable or unstable degree? **stable**

h. Define *Moderato*. **at a moderate speed**

i. Find and circle one accidental in this piece.

j. Name the interval at letter A. **maj 2**

k. Name the interval at letter B. **per 1**

© San Marco Publications 2018

Page 348, No. 1

Franz Schubert
Slumber Song

a. Add the time signature directly on the music.

b. Name the key of this piece. **G major**

c. Mark the phrases with slurs.

d. Label the phrases with *a*, *a¹*, and *b*.

e. Name the chord formed by the notes at A: **G major** B: **D major**

© San Marco Publications 2018

Page 349

1. Who composed the music shown above? **George Frideric Handel**

2. What is the name of the composition? **Messiah - Hallelujah Chorus**

3. What key is it in? **D major**

4. What four voices are used to sing this piece? **soprano alto tenor bass**

5. Name the triad formed by the notes at A **D major triad**

6. Name the interval at B. **per 4**

7. Name the interval at C. **maj 3**

8. Name the interval at D. **per 5**

Page 350

Sonatina

Cornelius Gurlitt
1820 -1901

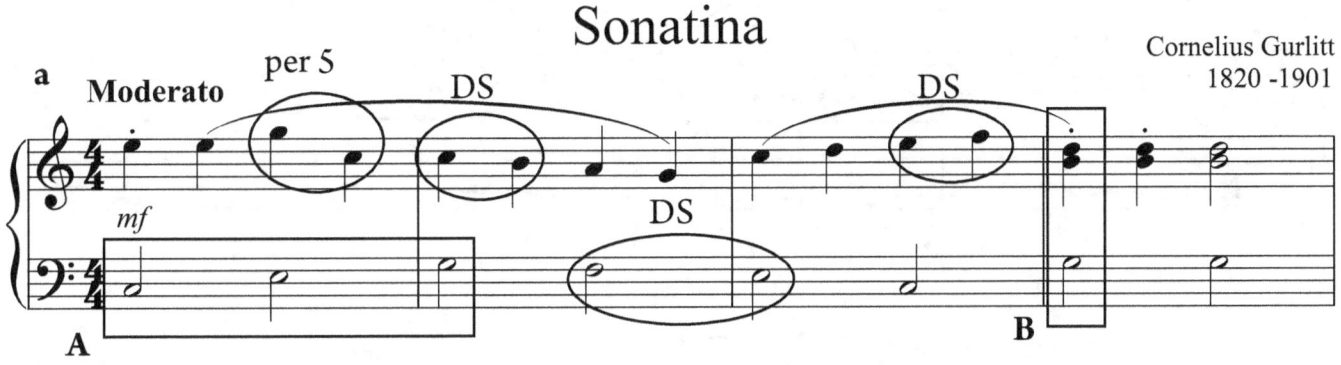

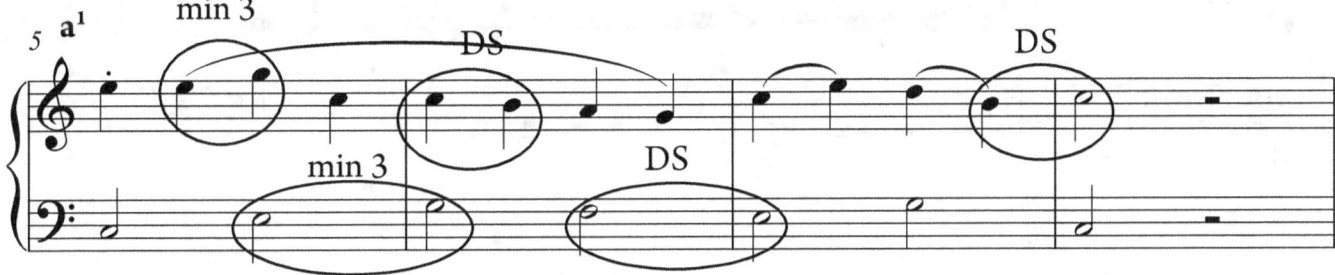

1. Name the composer of this piece? **Cornelius Gurlitt**

2. Name the key of this piece. **C major**

3. Write the time signature on the score.

4. Define "moderato" **at a moderate tempo or speed**

5. How many phrases are in this example? **2**

6. Does the first phrase end on a stable or unstable degree? **unstable**

7. Does the second phrase end on a stable or unstable degree? **stable**

8. Label the phrases either: (a - a¹⁾ or (a - b) depending on the form.

9. What triad is formed by the notes in the box at letter A: **C major triad**

10. What triad is formed by the notes in the box at letter B: **G major triad**

11. Find the interval of a harmonic major 3rd, circle it, and label it maj 3.

12. Find the interval of a melodic perfect 5th, circle it, and label it per 5.

13. Find two different diatonic semitones, circle them, and label them DS.

14. How many slurs occur in this piece? **5**

© San Marco Publications 2018

Page 351

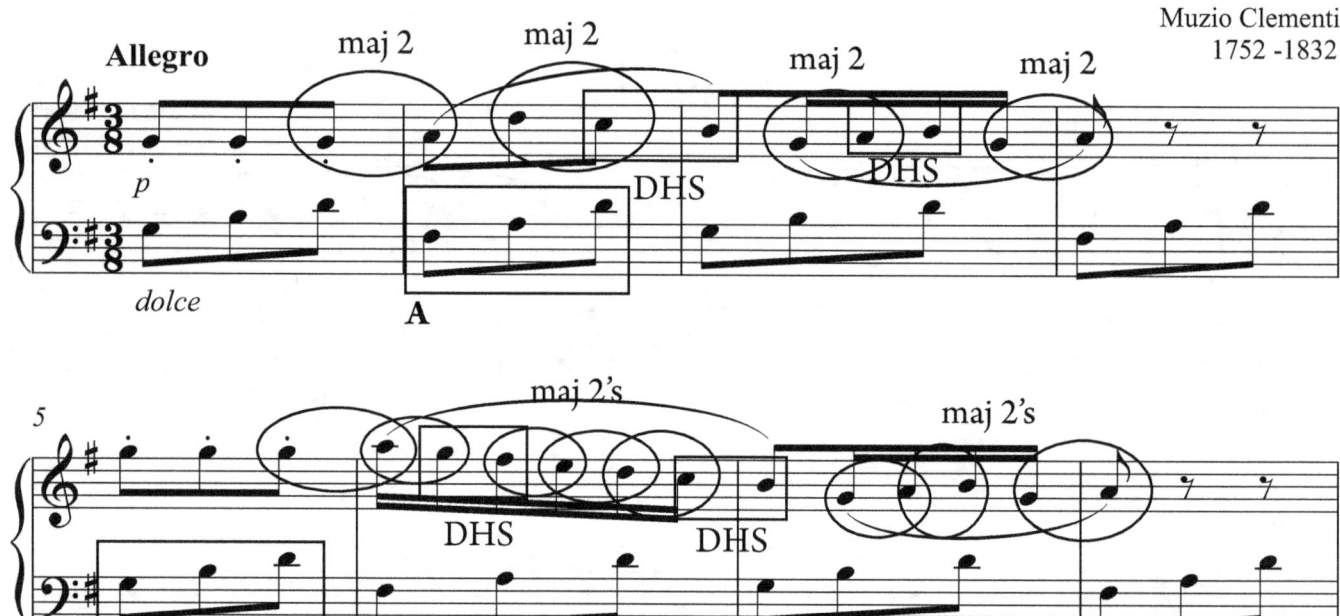

1. Name the composer of this piece? **Muzio Clementi**

2. When did he live? **1752-1832**

3. Write the time signature on the score.

4. Name the key of this piece. **G major**

5. Define "allegro." **fast**

6. Define "dolce." **sweetly**

7. For the triad at letter A, name the: Root **D**   Quality **major**   Inversion **1st**

8. For the triad at letter B, name the: Root **G**   Quality **major**   Inversion **root**

9. How many times does the broken tonic triad occur in the bass clef. **4**

10. Find a melodic major 2nd, circle it and label it maj 2.

11. Find a melodic major 3rd, circle it and label it maj 3.

12. Find a diatonic half step, put a box around it and label is DHS.

© San Marco Publications 2018

Page 352

1. Name the key of this piece? **F major**

2. Write the time signature on the score.

3. Check the terms that apply to this time signature. ☑compound ☐triple ☐simple ☑duple

4. Mark the phrases with a slur.

5. Label each phrase using the letters *a*, *a¹* or *b*.

6. Define "andantino." **a little faster than andante**

7. Name the triad at letter A.   root: **F**   quality: **major**

Page 355

Anton Diabelli
Op. 125. no. 3

1. Name the key of this piece. **C major**
2. Write the time signature directly on the score.
3. The form of this piece is: ☐ binary ☑ ternary
4. Label the score by using A, A¹, and B to define the form.
5. Define *Allegretto*. **fairly fast, a little slower than allegro**
6. Check all statements below that apply to the chord at A:

    ☑ tonic triad ☐ subdominant triad ☑ C major triad ☑ root position ☐ broken chord
7. Check all statements below that apply to the chord at B:

    ☐ tonic triad ☑ dominant triad ☑ G major triad ☐ 1st inversion ☑ solid or blocked chord
8. Name the cadence at C:

    ☑ perfect authentic cadence ☐ half cadence ☐ imperfect authentic cadence
9. Symbolize the chords of this cadence on the score using functional chord symbols.

Page 356

Anton Diabelli
Op. 125 No. 4

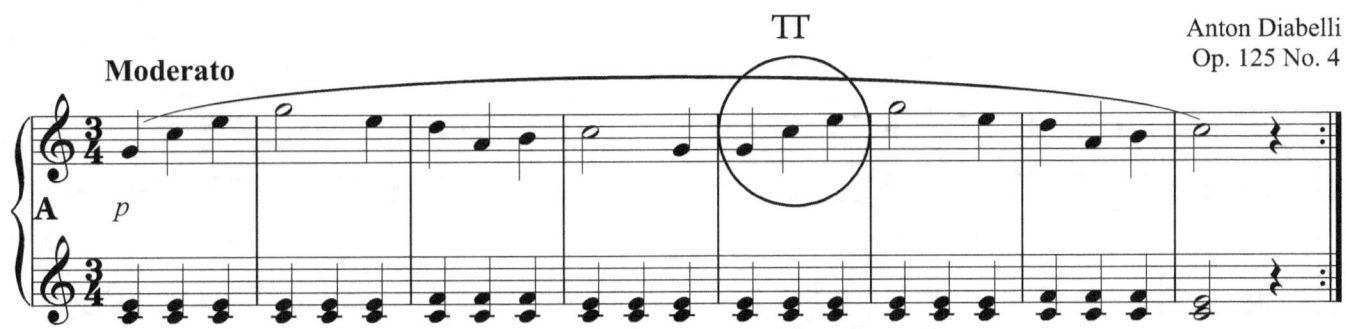

1. Name the key of this piece. **C major**

2. Write the time signature directly on the score.

3. Check the words below that apply to this time signature.

      ☑triple   ☐compound   ☐duple   ☑simple   ☐quadruple

4. Mark the phrases using a slur.

5. The form of this piece is: ☑binary   ☐ternary

6. Label the score by using A, A¹, and B to define the form.

7. Define *Moderato*. **at a moderate speed or tempo**

8. Name the chord at letter A: **G⁷, the dominant 7th**

9. For the chord at letter B name the: root **C**   quality **major**   position **2nd inv.**

10. For the chord at letter C name the: root **G**   quality **major**   position **root pos.**

11. The cadence at D is: ☐half   ☑perfect authentic   ☐imperfect authentic

12. Write the functional chord symbols for this cadence directly on the score.

13. Find and circle a broken dominant triad on the score. Label it DT.

14. Find and circle a broken tonic triad on the score. Label it TT.

© San Marco Publications 2018

Page 357

Joseph Haydn
(1732-1809)
Sonata Hob XVI 34, III

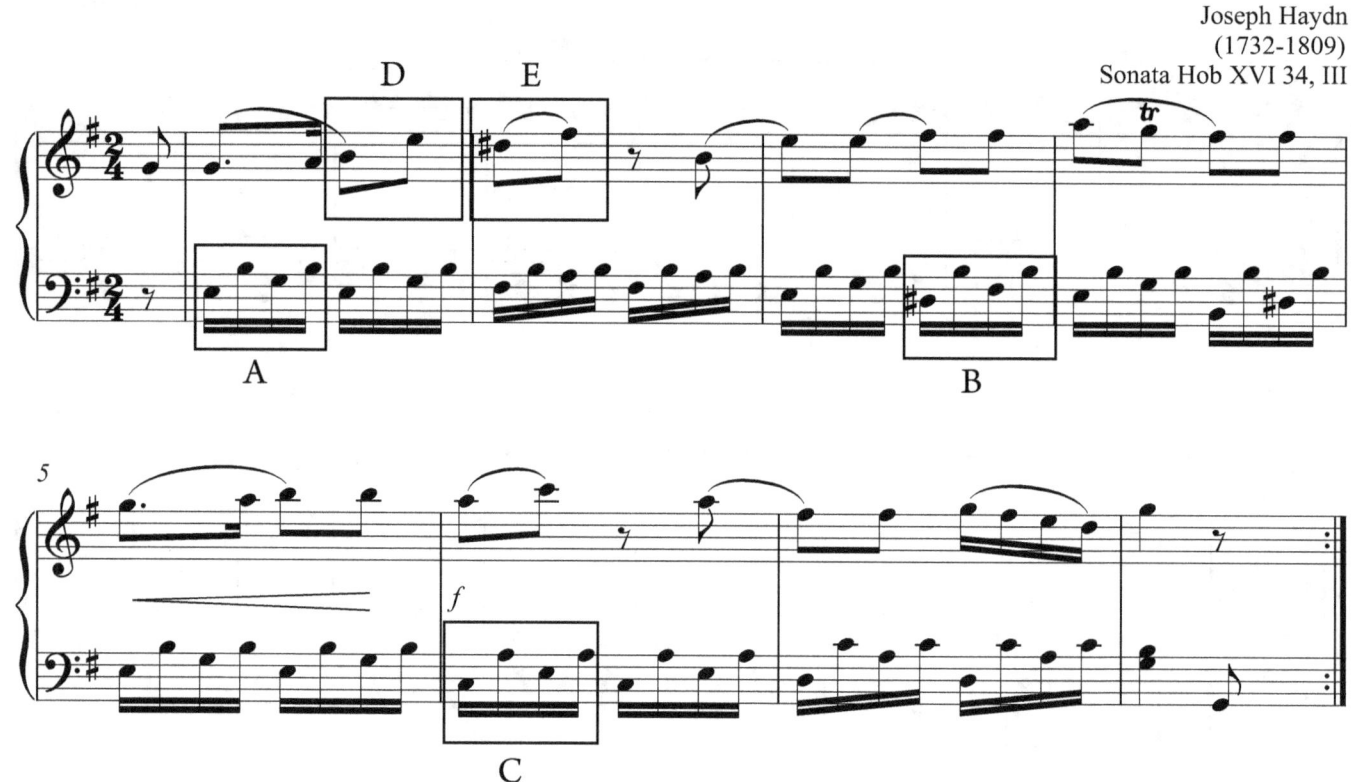

1. Name the key of this piece. **E minor**

2. Write the time signature directly on the score.

3. This excerpt is written for a right hand melody with left hand accompaniment. This is and example of:

    ❏polyphonic music ☑homophonic music ❏contrapuntal music ❏absolute music

4. What musical era was this piece composed? **Classical**

5. Name the chord at A: root **E**   quality **minor**   position **root pos**

6. Name the chord at B: root **B**   quality **major**   position **1st inv**

7. Name the chord at C: root **A**   quality **minor**   position **1st inv.**

8. In this piece, chord A is the: ☑tonic triad   ❏subdominant triad   ❏dominant triad

9. In this piece, chord B is the: ❏tonic triad   ❏subdominant triad   ☑dominant triad

10. In this piece, chord C is the: ❏tonic triad   ☑subdominant triad   ❏dominant triad

11. Define *Molto vivace*: **Very lively**

12. This excerpt is an example of a: ❏parallel period   ☑contrasting period

13. Name the interval at D: **min 3**

14. Name the interval at E: **per 4**

© San Marco Publications 2018

Page 360, No. 1

E minor:	V iv V i		B minor:	iv V i
F major:	I IV V		A minor:	iv V i
D minor:	iv V i		E major:	I IV V I
G♭ major:	I IV V I		G♯ minor:	i V i

Page 360, No. 2

1. tonic   2. dominant   3. subdominant   4. tonic

Page 361, No. 1

A major: I V V
C minor: i V iv

Page 362

1. Romantic era
2. A♭ major
3. 3/4
4. D♭ major
5. subdominant chord
6. E♭ major
7. dominant chord
8. C: neighbor tones   D: passing tones
9. fairly fast, a little slower than allegro
10. fortepiano, loud than suddenly soft
11. stable

George Frideric Handel
(1685 - 1759)

1. George Frideric Handel

2. Messiah

3. Baroque era

4. D minor

5. 3/2

6. simple triple time

7. tonic chord

8. dominant chord

9. subdominant chord

10. D: min 3rd   E: min 3rd   F: min 3rd

11. 4

12. 7

Page 364

Johannes Brahms
(1833-1897)
Weigenlied Op. 49 No. 4

1. E♭ major

2. 3/4

3. homophonic texture

4. Romantic era

5. Frédéric Chopin, Felix Mendelssohn, Robert Schumann, Pyotr Tchaikovsky, Franz Liszt

7. min 3

8. maj 3

9. dim 5

© San Marco Publications 2018

Page 366, No. 1

contrary	oblique	parallel	similar
oblique	parallel	contrary	parallel
similar	oblique	contrary	oblique

Page 367, No. 1

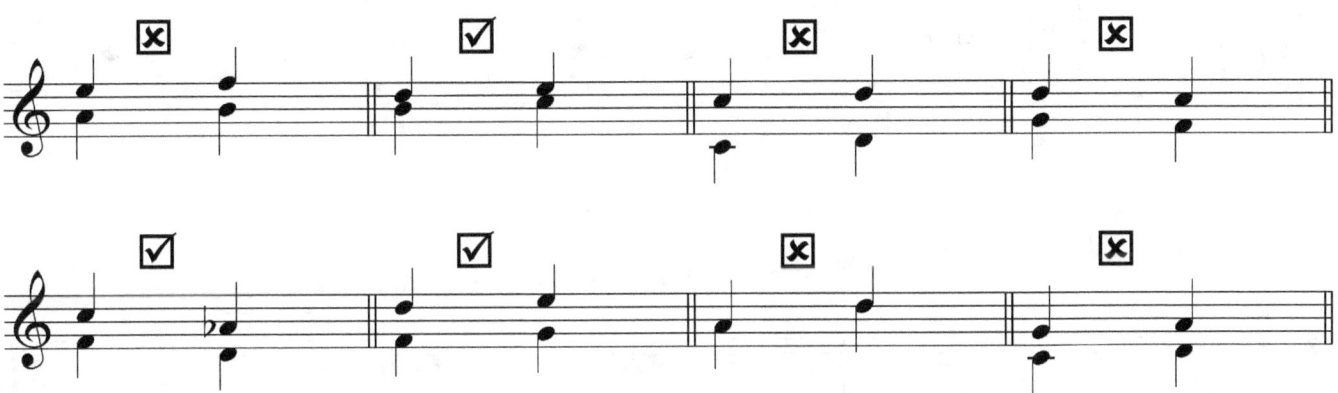

Page 367, No. 2

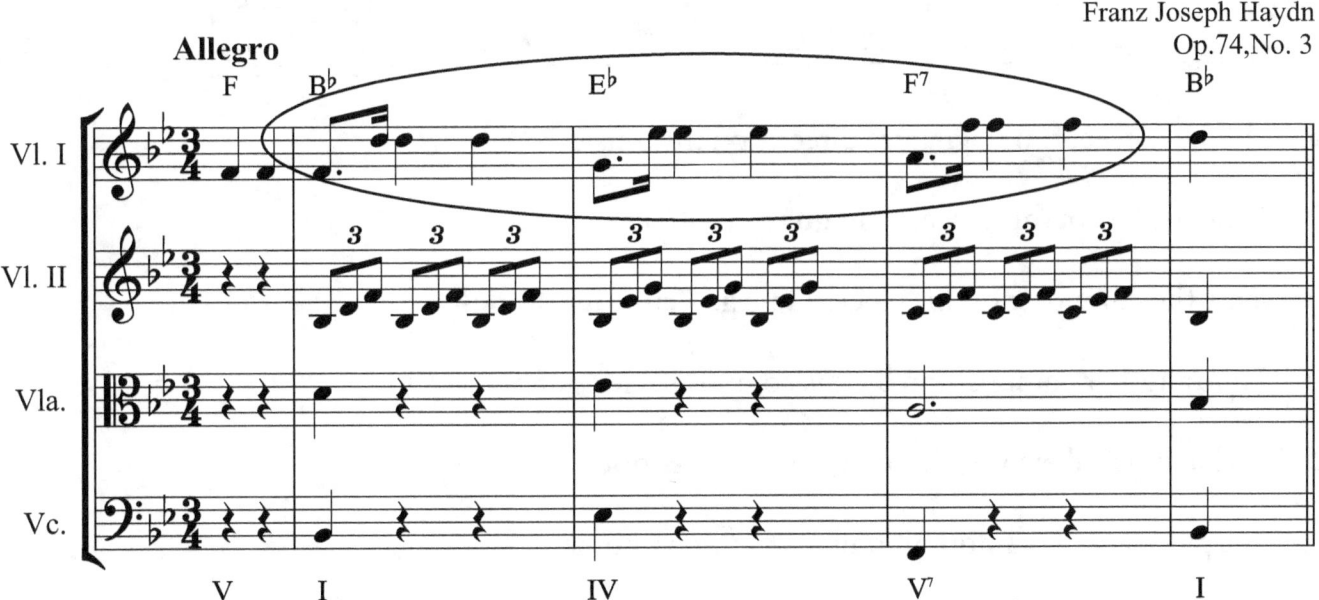

a. Name the key of this phrase. **B♭ major**
b. Write the time signature directly on the score. **3/4**
c. In what musical period was this piece composed? **Classical**
d. What open score is this written for? **String quartet**
e. State the implied harmony using functional and root/quality chord symbols on the score.
f. Find and circle a melodic sequence.
g. Name the cadence at the end of this phrase. **Imperfect authentic**

© San Marco Publications 2018

Passepied

George Frideric Handel
(1685-1759)

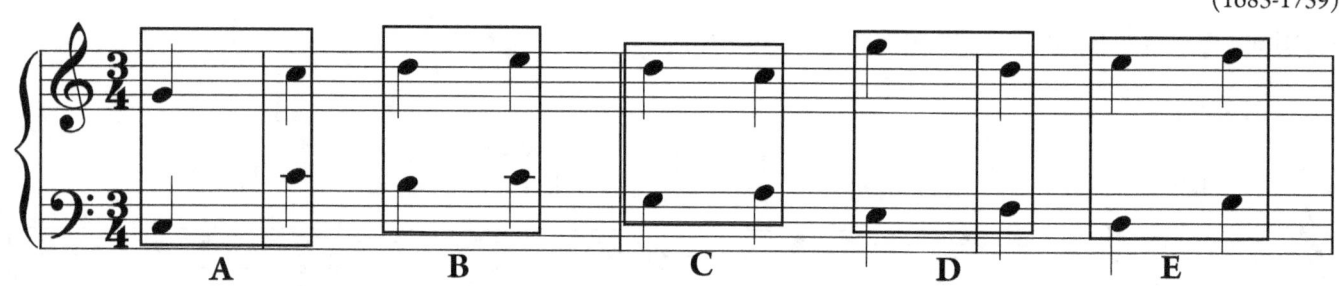

a. Add the correct time signature directly on the music. **3/4**

b. Name the key of this piece. **C major**

c. Name the composer of this piece. **George Frideric Handel**

d. Name another composition by this composer. **Messiah**

d. In what musical era was this composed? **Baroque**

e. This piece is: ☐ monophonic   ☑ polyphonic

f. Identify the motion at:

A:	☐ contrary	☐ parallel	☑ similar	☐ oblique
B:	☐ contrary	☑ parallel	☐ similar	☐ oblique
C:	☑ contrary	☐ parallel	☐ similar	☐ oblique
D:	☑ contrary	☐ parallel	☐ similar	☐ oblique
E:	☐ contrary	☐ parallel	☑ similar	☐ oblique
F:	☐ contrary	☐ parallel	☐ similar	☑ oblique